Nutrient-Dense Meal Prep

Quick and Easy Recipes to Heal Your Gut, Balance Your Hormones
and Help You Adopt a Healthier Diet and Lifestyle

Olivia Robertson-Moe, NTP

of [R]evolve Primal Health

PAGE STREET
PUBLISHING CO.

PAGE STREET
PUBLISHING CO.

First published in 2024 by
Page Street Publishing Co.
27 Congress Street, Suite 1511
Salem, MA 01970
www.pagestreetpublishing.com

Distributed by Macmillan, sales in Canada by The Canadian Manda Group.

28 27 26 25 24   1 2 3 4 5

ISBN-13: 978-1-64567-856-4
ISBN-10: 1-64567-856-3

Library of Congress Control Number: 2023936759

Cover and book design by Molly Kate Young for Page Street Publishing Co.
Photography by Anne Watson

Printed and bound in the United States of America

To my mom and dad—thanks for teaching me my love for food and an even greater love for the planet.

Contents

Foreword by Diana Rodgers, RD   6

Introduction   8
What Is "Nutrient Dense"?   9
Tips for Sourcing Ingredients   9
Your Meal Prep Guide   13

5 Weeks of Meal Plans   15

Easy-Prep Proteins   27
15-Minute Chicken Liver Mousse   29
Simplified Bone Broth   30
Turmeric Pickled Eggs   33
Easy Roasted Chicken   34
Simple Curry Chicken Salad   37
Nutrient-Rich Liver Meatballs   38
My Hearty Organ Meat Chili   41
Thai Larb Lettuce Cups   42
Nourishing Beef Heart Jerky   45
Comforting Short Rib Ragu   46
Beef Tongue Birria   49
Make-and-Freeze Kebabs   52
Family-Size Pork Carnitas   55
Batched Shepherd's Pie   56
Seafood Red Curry   59
Maple Salmon Bites   60

Healthier Carbohydrates   63
Gluten-Free Sourdough
Sandwich Bread   65
Cheesy Scalloped Potatoes   66
Prebiotic Potato Salad   69
Middle Eastern Lentil Salad   70
Winter Squash Mash   73
Gut-Friendly Herb Rice   74
Fresh Corn Tortillas   77
Creamy Squash Soup   78

Versatile Veggies   81
Perfect Roasted Veggies   83
Easy 30-Minute Sauerkraut   84
Lacto-Fermented Veggies   87
Bone Broth Braised Greens   88
Rustic French Ratatouille   91
Heart-Healthy Beet Salad   92
Simple Dill Carrot Salad   95

Protein-Rich Breakfasts   97
Single-Serving Frittata   99
Mini Meat Muffins   100
Balanced Smoothie Formula   103
   Blueberry Cheesecake Smoothie   *103*
   Vitamin C–Avocado Smoothie   *103*
5-Minute Bone Broth Breakfast Soup   104
Savory Masa Bowl   107
Make-Ahead Protein Oatmeal   108
Breakfast Fried Rice   111
Cottage Cheese Breakfast Parfait   112
High-Protein Pancakes   115
Clean-the-Fridge Omelet   116

Decadent (and Nutrient-Dense!) Desserts 119

High-Protein Pot de Crème 121

Creamy Nutrient-Dense Ice Cream 122

Gut-Healing Maple Marshmallows 125

Hormone-Balancing Chocolate Truffles 126

Freezer-Friendly Mint Truffles 129

Grain-Free Frosted Pumpkin Bread 130

Gluten-Free Fermented Banana Bread 133

Grain-Free Chocolate Chip Cookies 134

Make-Ahead Hot Chocolate Bombs 137

Single-Serving Key Lime Pie 138

Sauces and Condiments 141

5-Ingredient Mayonnaise 143

Probiotic-Rich Salsa 144

Spicy Cilantro Sauce 147

Everyday Vinaigrette Dressing 148

Probiotic-Rich Salad Dressing 150

Creamy Caesar Dip 151

Budget-Friendly Pesto 153

Simple Fruit Jam 154

Bone Marrow Butter 157

Chimichurri 158

Fermented Hot Sauce 161

Acknowledgments 162

About the Author 162

Index 163

Foreword

Unless you've been living under a rock, you know that we're sicker today than we've ever been before and the majority of our issues are coming from our diets. The center of our grocery stores is now an ultraprocessed circus show, with exploding flavor combinations that encourage us to overeat. Yet these foods are void of the true forms of nutrients that our bodies are designed to function on. And it's not your fault. Big food companies and even mainstream nutritionists are telling you that this stuff in boxes is what you should be eating, even if they say to just eat less of it.

I'm here to tell you, that stuff isn't food. It's profits for corporations and shareholders who don't care about your health at all. It's time to get back to basics and relearn what our grandmothers and great-grandmothers knew—that real food, cooked from scratch, is the best way to health.

Olivia has been my right-hand woman, helping me with my social media and with my nonprofit, the Global Food Justice Alliance, where we educate people about the importance of nutrient-dense, animal-sourced foods. We also help increase access to meat for underserved communities and influence the meat industry to be more sustainable. Olivia is not only a diligent employee but is truly dedicated to making sure people know how to prepare these important foods—a skill most have forgotten in our modern, grab-and-go, convenience culture.

As a "real food" dietitian who is pushing back hard against the movement to eat less meat, I am 100 percent behind what Olivia has to tell you in this book. Nutrient density is where it's at. It's not about calories or carbs or meat or plants . . . it's about getting the RIGHT combination of nutrients—vitamins, minerals and fatty acids. This is where the Paleo, or "real food" movement started, but somehow it seemed to get hijacked by those who had certain agendas to push. But at the heart of it, the #JERF—"just eat real food"—idea had it right all along.

And beyond nutrients, making sure you're getting the right levels of these vitamins, minerals and fats in your diet is essential. That's where working with someone who is trained is so important. Olivia and I are both trained nutritional therapy practitioners (NTPs) who know that bone broth, butter, some roasted veggies and a steak beat out what typical nutritionists are trying to tell you. See, they'll say that as long as you're undereating calories, you're on a great "diet." But life isn't about restriction and eating food packaged in cardboard boxes . . . to me, it's about enjoying real food, cooked from scratch, that nourishes the cells in your body and brain to give you optimal health.

Olivia is a wiz in the kitchen, and her recipes are not only healthy and delicious, but approachable for those just getting started on their journey. Unlike other cookbooks with complicated instructions and exotic ingredients, *Nutrient-Dense Meal Prep* makes it easy and simple to eat well. It covers everything from sourcing groceries to meal plans, and it will teach you to make this way of eating a sustainable part of your life from here on out.

So, dig in; indulge yourself, your family and your friends in optimal health through tasty and nourishing meals; and if you'd like to learn more about the work Olivia and I are doing at Global Food Justice Alliance, visit www.globalfoodjustice.org.

Diana Rodgers, RD

Diana Rodgers

Introduction

Welcome to *Nutrient-Dense Meal Prep*, your guide to sourcing, preparing and creating a nutrient-dense diet with minimal stress. I have seen firsthand the power that food has in healing some of the most common health issues. My journey with nutrition and food started with my own health problems. For years, I struggled with severe digestive issues and hormone imbalances that impacted my skin, mood and energy. I tried every diet under the sun to heal my digestive issues and problematic skin—vegetarian, vegan, gluten-free, dairy-free and fat-free (all the "frees"). Restrictive dieting only made my health problems worse and damaged my relationship with food.

When I finally went back to the basics—sourcing quality animal foods and seasonal produce and learning traditional techniques for preparing food—I finally felt relief from my symptoms. I said good-bye to restrictive diets, and hello to real, nutrient-rich food. Instead of endless kale salads, I learned to properly prepare my food with traditional techniques, such as slow cooking, soaking and fermenting, and how to incorporate nutrient-dense foods. I learned to source my food in ways that increase their nutrient value *and* support the environment. With these changes, I went from sick and tired to energetic and thriving. My chronic stomach issues went away, I have natural energy and steady moods, my skin slowly healed and I have an amazing relationship with food.

Once I saw the wonders that diet and lifestyle changes can make, I became a nutritional therapy practitioner to help others heal their gut and balance their hormones naturally through nutrition. Now, I want to teach you how to reach optimal health, all from the comfort of your kitchen.

The problem is, most people lead busy lives and don't have the time to cook three meals a day from scratch. Do you stay on track with nutrient-dense eating and feel great for a week or two before you become overwhelmed and throw in the towel on home cooking? If so, you need to master this one skill: meal prepping! I created this book of 60 large-batch, freezer-friendly meals to help you stay consistent with a nutrient-dense diet without the stress of time-consuming cooking.

My goal was to make this your everyday book full of simple recipes that don't require many specialty items or long ingredients lists. I hope these delicious dishes help you achieve your best health yet!

What Is "Nutrient Dense"?

Nutrient density refers to the concentration of micronutrients (vitamins and minerals) and amino acids (the building blocks of protein) in a food.

A nutrient-dense diet prioritizes nutrient-rich foods, such as meat, organ meat, seafood, a variety of seasonal fruits and veggies, starchy veggies and whole food carbs, and minimizes inflammatory foods, such as industrial seed oils, processed foods and refined carbs, including flour, pasta and excess sugars.

My approach to a nutrient-dense diet means focusing on real, whole foods that nourish *you*. This can take a bit of self-experimentation to understand what works best for you—for some people, this may mean including properly prepared grains and dairy, whereas others may choose to avoid those—everyone is different. Part of finding the optimal diet for you is trying new things out!

You may think you're consuming loads of nutrients if you're eating a plant-rich diet, but because of the depletion of soil over the past few decades, our food is no longer as nutritious as it once was. Plus, plant foods lack some of the essential nutrients that we need to thrive, such as heme iron, zinc, vitamin B_{12} and omega-3 fatty acids. We also need to consider bioavailability of nutrients—how easily the nutrient can be absorbed and utilized by your body. For example, nonheme iron found in plant foods is less easily absorbed than heme iron, which is found only in animal foods. The omega-3 fats in such plant foods as walnuts is ALA, which requires an inefficient conversion process to important forms of omega-3 fats EPA and DHA, or we can get EPA and DHA straight from such animal foods as fatty fish. That's why the recipes in this book focus on sourcing the most nutrient-rich foods, including meat, organ meat and seasonal produce, and learning to prepare food in a way that increases the availability of nutrients—for instance, fermenting grains and veggies to improve digestibility.

Don't worry—my approach to a nutrient-dense diet doesn't mean every meal has to be meat heavy or have hidden liver in it. You can even make desserts that are minimally and naturally sweetened, packed with healthy fats and added protein to improve satiety, and use real food ingredients that are delicious and leave you feeling amazing!

Tips for Sourcing Ingredients

Learning how to source quality ingredients makes your food taste better, saves you money and is a great way to support local farmers and the environment.

When it comes to sourcing ingredients, buy the best you can afford—even when it comes to such animal foods as meat, dairy and eggs. These are nutrient-rich foods and you shouldn't feel the need to avoid them if the highest-quality items are not in your budget. Food labels can be confusing, so here is a quick cheat sheet to help you prioritize what to look for.

	Best	Better	Avoid/Limit
Red Meat	local, regeneratively raised, 100% grass-fed, organic	organic, grass-fed/grain-finished	conventional, grain-fed
Pork	heritage breed, pasture-raised from a local farm, corn- & soy-free	organic	conventional, industrial CAFO* pork
Poultry & Eggs	pasture-raised from a local farm	organic, free-range	conventional, industrial CAFO poultry
Seafood	wild, line-caught, local, smaller fish	sustainably farmed, antibiotic-free	farmed, larger fish

Concentrated Animal Feeding Operation

I hope that my recipes for bulk cooking and using more affordable cuts of meat, combined with the following tips for sourcing ingredients, can help you get top-notch groceries in your budget, but always do what is best for you and your situation.

Meat

- **Find a good source:** Look for 100% grass-fed and finished, pasture-raised meat, but as I said earlier, buy the best you can afford. You can use an online resource, such as eatwild.com or farmmatch.com, to find a local farm or butcher that sources locally. If you have a farmers' market near you, connect with local farms there. If there is no local farm available to you, check your local grocery store or food co-op, or explore the many farms or services that ship grass-fed meat to your door, such as White Oak Pastures, Force of Nature Meats or ButcherBox®.

- **Buy in bulk:** Once you have a reliable, quality source, look for an affordable buying option. Buying in bulk is the most cost-effective way to source quality meat. Many farms offer the ability to buy meat in bulk—⅛ cow, ¼ cow, ½ cow, etc. Get a chest freezer and fill it up with quality meat! When I buy meat in bulk from my local farm, my meat costs as low as $5 per pound (455 g), cheaper than many conventional meats in supermarkets. So, if a larger up-front invest-ment works for you, look for opportunities to buy a full animal, half an animal or split the purchase with neighbors or family (be sure to ask for all parts of the animal—organs, bones, fat, etc.).

- **Opt for larger cuts of meat:** Aside from buying in bulk, it's important to opt for full cuts of meat—both for nutritional and financial reasons. When we choose large cuts of meat, such as beef chuck instead of a rib eye or a full chicken instead of chicken breasts, the options are typically cheaper and also provide more nutrients.

- **Eat nose to tail:** Eating or using every part of the animal is the best way to get the most nutrients at an affordable price. A lot of times, organ meats, bones or other nonmuscle meats are less common ingredients and therefore cheaper. A common mistake that many health-conscious people make is to eat only muscle meat. When we consume only muscle meat, not only are we spending a lot more money, but we miss out on many nutritional benefits from other areas of the animal—such as collagen, which is critical for gut, skin and joint health.

Dairy

- **Source quality dairy:** Most people, including myself, have been led to believe that dairy is not a healthy food. That could not be further from the truth. While dairy is not required for a nutrient-dense diet, dairy products are a great source of bioavailable nutrients, including calcium, protein, vitamin D, potassium and phosphorus. Like most things, it's the quality of the dairy that matters. Most milk products that you find in the grocery store are pasteurized, meaning they have been heated to a high temperature that can impact the nutrient composition. Pasteurization also destroys digestive enzymes naturally present in milk, which can impact digestibility. Raw milk is simply unpasteurized dairy, meaning the digestive enzymes are intact, so some people who cannot digest dairy tolerate raw dairy better. Check out getrawmilk.com or rawmilkinstitute.org to locate quality raw dairy near you. Most grocery stores also carry raw cheese, especially Gruyère and Parmesan. While raw dairy is not inherently unsafe, it is very important to obtain it from a trustworthy source with sanitary production and rigorous testing processes. If you can't find raw milk and you can tolerate pasteurized dairy, it is still a great source of essential nutrients. Look for low-temperature pasteurized and non-homogenized dairy in the store. Kalona SuperNatural® is a brand of organic low-temperature pasteurized, non-homogenized milk from pasture-raised cows available in some grocery stores. I also recommend prioritizing local, grass-fed, organic dairy when possible.

- **Try fermented options:** Did you know that dairy can be fermented? It can! In fact, many of your favorite dairy products, such as yogurt and kefir, are fermented. Many cheeses are also fermented! The fermentation process breaks down milk proteins and lactose, so some people who have trouble digesting dairy can tolerate fermented dairy products better.

- **Experiment with A2 dairy:** Have you started noticing A2 dairy labels on grocery shelves? But what *is* A2 dairy? Most cow milk contains A1 beta-casein and A2 beta-casein. The A1 protein may be difficult for some people to digest, so some brands are beginning to produce cow's milk with only A2 proteins, which can be easier to digest. Goat and sheep dairy products are also great options, since they naturally contain only A2 beta-casein, which is why some people can tolerate goat and sheep dairy items better than cow's milk. Alexandre Family Farm® produces organic, regenerative 100% A2 dairy, so look out for it in a grocery store near you.

Produce

- **Eat local and seasonal:** Seasonal produce is the fruits and vegetables available during different months of the year based on temperature variation. Defining "local food" is pretty arbitrary and ultimately what is local food comes down to your judgment. Two ways that I define local food are: (1) food purchased directly from the farmer, or (2) food produced in a similar environment to the one you are living or staying in. There are a few reasons that I recommend shopping for local, seasonal produce:

    - **Nutrition:** Shopping for fruits and veggies that are grown close to you and in season will be fresher, taste better and may be richer in nutrients. Fruit from a farm local to you will be picked when ripe, rather than a pineapple that has been picked while unripe and shipped across the world and ripen off the plant. While that's not to say that nonlocal fruits and veggies are not nutritious, seasonal eating can help you get a more varied diet—and more variety in your diet means a wider variety of micronutrients.

    - **Affordable:** Purchasing local and seasonal produce is usually cheaper than buying those same fruits and vegetables in their off-season. When fruits and veggies are produced locally, much of the transportation costs are cut out, and they are often in large supply, so they can be sold at lower prices.

    - **Good for the planet:** Maybe most important, shopping for seasonal and local produce is an effective way to support the environment. When you buy local produce, you are usually supporting smaller farms that are stewarding land in a sustainable or even regenerative fashion to support biodiversity and soil health. The best way to eat locally and seasonally is by purchasing directly from farmers when and if possible. Check out eatwild.com or farmmatch.com, or Google a farmers' market in your area. To shop seasonally at grocery stores, familiarize yourself with what is in season and check the produce tag to see where the crop comes from!

- **Utilize Community Supported Agriculture (CSA):** Find a farm that offers regular (usually weekly) deliveries of locally grown farm products during one or more harvest season(s) on a subscription or membership basis. A great place to check whether these are in your area is by visiting ams.usda.gov and going to its Local Food section.

- **Look for a local co-op:** If you don't have access to farmers' markets, CSA programs or local farms, search for a health food market or co-op in your area.

- **Start a garden:** Whether you have a huge backyard or a windowsill in an apartment, you can grow your own food. This is the best way to have the freshest seasonal food. Grab some herb seedlings—such as basil, mint and thyme—and grow them in pots on a sunny windowsill!

Your Meal Prep Guide

My Easy Approach to Meal Prep

I used to hate meal prepping. It was overwhelming and time consuming, and by day three, I was sick of my large, batched meal and I would ditch it for takeout. By shifting the meal prep approach away from cooking one large portion of a single dish to cooking a few staples to stock the fridge for the week, you can save money and time, as well as reduce food waste.

Carve out a couple of hours during the week—this is typically on a weekend for most people, but whatever works for your schedule—and prep one to three proteins, one or two carbohydrates and one or two vegetable dishes. Depending on your schedule, you can also prep breakfasts that are ready to eat or easy to pack and take on the go. I've scheduled five weekly meal plans (see page 15), but you can always mix and match recipes in this book on your own if you want to follow your own menu and routine. Then, throughout the week, you can create a variety of meals using your prepared dishes, instead of eating lasagna for four days in a row. You will also find easy sauce and condiment recipes (page 141) that you can stock in your fridge for an easy way to switch up flavors.

Must-Have Meal Prep Tools

Glass and stainless-steel containers: I recommend storing your food in glass or stainless steel, rather than plastic, as much as possible. Invest in some Mason jars of varying sizes to use for fermentation vessels, on-the-go breakfasts and general food storage. Store in glass containers any food that you will want to microwave. Pyrex bowls are also a great tool because you can use them to make the dish, and then just add a lid and store it directly in the bowl, no extra cleanup required.

Portioned freezer trays: It's important to be able to divide food into single portions so you can thaw the exact amount that you want to reheat. My go-tos are Souper Cubes® trays. They are made of food-grade silicone so that you can easily pop out the food once it's frozen and store it in a gallon-sized (3.8-L) ziplock bag or other container. It is great for reducing food waste. Souper Cubes also offers smaller trays that are helpful for making truffles and other desserts in this book.

Dutch oven or slow cooker: An oven-safe pot, such as a Dutch oven, or a slow cooker or pressure cooker will make meal prep a breeze. They are great tools for "set it and forget it" hands-off meals—for example, braising large cuts of meats at a low temperature for many hours, for a big batch of tender protein.

5 Weeks of Meal Plans

I have put together a few five-day meal plans to get you started on this new approach to nutrient-dense meal prep. If it helps you to have every meal planned out, go ahead and follow them, or feel free to make them your own depending on your schedule and needs—maybe you need to prep all your breakfasts and lunches but enjoy cooking dinner a few nights per week. Experiment and find what works best for you! I typically recommend using the weekends to use up any leftovers or go out to eat with friends. I find that's a more intuitive way of meal prepping!

Week 1

Breakfast #1: Single-Serving Frittata (page 99)

Breakfast #2: Blueberry Cheesecake Smoothie (page 103)

Protein #1: Simple Curry Chicken Salad (page 37)

Protein #2: Easy Roasted Chicken (page 34)

Protein #3: Thai Larb Lettuce Cups (page 42)

Carb #1: Gluten-Free Sourdough Sandwich Bread (page 65)

Veggie #1: Bone Broth Braised Greens (page 88)

Snack #1: Nourishing Beef Heart Jerky (page 45)

Dessert #1: Freezer-Friendly Mint Truffles (page 129)

Dessert #2: Hormone-Balancing Chocolate Truffles (page 126)

Suggested Schedule

	Breakfast	Lunch	Snack (optional)	Dinner	Dessert (optional)
Sunday	Finish leftovers from the prior week.	Use up leftovers or go out to lunch!		Easy Roasted Chicken w/Bone Broth Braised Greens	Leftovers from the prior week.
Monday	Blueberry Cheesecake Smoothie	Simple Curry Chicken Salad w/ Gluten-Free Sourdough Sandwich Bread & Bone Broth Braised Greens	Nourishing Beef Heart Jerky	Thai Larb Lettuce Cups	Freezer-Friendly Mint Truffles
Tuesday	Single-Serving Frittata	Thai Larb Lettuce Cups	Nourishing Beef Heart Jerky	Easy Roasted Chicken w/ Bone Broth Braised Greens	Hormone-Balancing Chocolate Truffles
Wednesday	Blueberry Cheesecake Smoothie	Simple Curry Chicken Salad w/ Gluten-Free Sourdough Sandwich Bread & Bone Broth Braised Greens	Nourishing Beef Heart Jerky	Thai Larb Lettuce Cups	Freezer-Friendly Mint Truffles
Thursday	Single-Serving Frittata	Simple Curry Chicken Salad w/ Gluten-Free Sourdough Sandwich Bread & Bone Broth Braised Greens	Nourishing Beef Heart Jerky	Thai Larb Lettuce Cups	Hormone-Balancing Chocolate Truffles
Friday	Blueberry Cheesecake Smoothie	Thai Larb Lettuce Cups	Nourishing Beef Heart Jerky	Easy Roasted Chicken & Bone Broth Braised Greens	Freezer-Friendly Mint Truffles
Saturday	Enjoy a big brunch with remaining frittata, leftover chicken and any other leftovers.			Finish up any leftovers of Thai Larb Lettuce Cups.	Freezer-Friendly Mint Truffles

Meal Prep Schedule

Starting Notes

- Two days before your first meal prep day, you will want to start the sourdough fermenting process.

- One day before your first meal prep day, generously salt the chicken and stick it back in the fridge.

Meal Prep Day #1

- Begin by making the Nourishing Beef Heart Jerky (page 45) so that it can spend time dehydrating while you prep the other dishes.

- Prepare the Gluten-Free Sourdough Sandwich Bread dough (page 65) and bake it.

- Once the jerky is dehydrating and the bread is baking, start to prepare the Easy Roasted Chicken (page 34) by removing the full chicken from the fridge to let it come up to room temperature for about an hour.

- While the chicken is resting on the counter, portion out the ingredients you will need for your Blueberry Cheesecake Smoothies (page 103) during the week.

- Once the bread is out of the oven, season your chicken and bake it. While the chicken bakes, prepare all the ingredients for the Simple Curry Chicken Salad (page 37) and make the Bone Broth Braised Greens (page 88).

- Once the chicken is done cooking, carve the bird and store the meat, using the chicken breast to complete the Simple Curry Chicken Salad (page 37).

Meal Prep Day #2

- Monday night, start by making the Single-Serving Frittata (page 99). While the frittata bakes, make the Thai Larb Lettuce Cups (page 42).

- This is also a great time to make the Freezer-Friendly Mint Truffles (page 129) and Hormone-Balancing Chocolate Truffles (page 126).

Week 2

Breakfast #1: 5-Minute Bone Broth Breakfast Soup (page 104)

Breakfast #2: Mini Meat Muffins (page 100)

Protein #1: Maple Salmon Bites (page 60)

Protein #2: Make-and-Freeze Kebabs (page 52)

Protein #3: Batched Shepherd's Pie (page 56)

Carb #1: Gut-Friendly Herb Rice (page 74)

Veggie #1: Lacto-Fermented Veggies (page 87)

Snack #1: Turmeric Pickled Eggs (page 33)

Dessert #1: Make-Ahead Hot Chocolate Bombs (page 137)

Dessert #2: High-Protein Pot de Crème (page 121)

Suggested Schedule

	Breakfast	Lunch	Snack (optional)	Dinner	Dessert (optional)
Sunday	Finish leftovers from the prior week.	Use up leftovers or go out to lunch!		Maple Salmon Bites w/ Gut-Friendly Herb Rice & Lacto-Fermented Veggies	Use up leftovers from previous week.
Monday	Mini Meat Muffins	Maple Salmon Bites w/ Gut-Friendly Herb Rice & Lacto-Fermented Veggies	Turmeric Pickled Eggs	Make-and-Freeze Kebabs w/ Gut-Friendly Herb Rice	High-Protein Pot de Crème
Tuesday	5-Minute Bone Broth Breakfast Soup	Make-and-Freeze Kebabs w/ Gut-Friendly Herb Rice	Mini Meat Muffins	Maple Salmon Bites w/ Gut-Friendly Herb Rice & Lacto-Fermented Veggies	High-Protein Pot de Crème
Wednesday	Mini Meat Muffins	Maple Salmon Bites w/ Gut-Friendly Herb Rice & Lacto-Fermented Veggies	Turmeric Pickled Eggs	Batched Shepherd's Pie	Make-Ahead Hot Chocolate Bombs
Thursday	5-Minute Bone Broth Breakfast Soup	Batched Shepherd's Pie	Mini Meat Muffins	Make-and-Freeze Kebabs w/ Gut-Friendly Herb Rice	High-Protein Pot de Crème
Friday	Mini Meat Muffins	Make-and-Freeze Kebabs w/ Gut-Friendly Herb Rice	Turmeric Pickled Eggs	Batched Shepherd's Pie	Make-Ahead Hot Chocolate Bombs
Saturday	5-Minute Bone Broth Breakfast Soup	Batched Shepherd's Pie	High-Protein Pot de Crème	Finish up any leftovers!	Make-Ahead Hot Chocolate Bombs

Meal Prep Schedule

Starting Notes

- This week includes Lacto-Fermented Veggies (page 87), which need to be prepared a few weeks in advance. I recommend that you make a few batches to have on hand in your fridge.

- Three to six hours before you start cooking, begin the process of soaking the Gut-Friendly Herb Rice (page 74).

Meal Prep Day #1

- Drain, cook and prepare the rice. While the rice cooks, prepare the Mini Meat Muffins (page 100).

- Boil the eggs and prepare the Turmeric Pickled Eggs (page 33).

- Prepare the Make-and-Freeze Kebabs (page 52). I also recommend you make the Spicy Cilantro Sauce (page 147) to serve with the kebabs.

- If you don't have bone broth, make a batch to have on hand for the 5-Minute Bone Broth Breakfast Soup (page 104).

- Prepare the Maple Salmon Bites (page 60) for dinner and store the leftovers for future lunches and dinners. Prepare the High-Protein Pot de Crème (page 121) and portion it out for the week.

Meal Prep Day #2

- On Wednesday evening, prepare the Batched Shepherd's Pie (page 56) for dinner and store the leftovers. Prepare the Make-Ahead Hot Chocolate Bombs (page 137) as well.

Week 3

Breakfast #1: Clean-the-Fridge Omelet (page 116)

Breakfast #2: Vitamin C–Avocado Smoothie (page 103)

Protein #1: Beef Tongue Birria (page 49)

Protein #2: Seafood Red Curry (page 59)

Protein #3: Family-Size Pork Carnitas (page 55)

Veggie #1: Perfect Roasted Veggies (page 83)

Carb #1: Fresh Corn Tortillas (page 77)

Snack #1: Simplified Bone Broth (page 30)

Dessert #1: Creamy Nutrient-Dense Ice Cream (page 122)

Dessert #2: Grain-Free Chocolate Chip Cookies (page 134)

Suggested Schedule

	Breakfast	Lunch	Snack (optional)	Dinner	Dessert (optional)
Sunday	Finish leftovers from the prior week.	Use up leftovers or go out to lunch!		Seafood Red Curry	Use up leftovers from previous week.
Monday	Vitamin C–Avocado Smoothie	Seafood Red Curry	Simplified Bone Broth	Family-Size Pork Carnitas w/Fresh Corn Tortillas & Perfect Roasted Veggies	Creamy Nutrient-Dense Ice Cream
Tuesday	Vitamin C–Avocado Smoothie	Seafood Red Curry	Simplified Bone Broth	Beef Tongue Birria w/Fresh Corn Tortillas & Perfect Roasted Veggies	Grain-Free Chocolate Chip Cookies
Wednesday	Clean-the-Fridge Omelet	Beef Tongue Birria w/Fresh Corn Tortillas & Perfect Roasted Veggies	Simplified Bone Broth	Family-Size Pork Carnitas w/Fresh Corn Tortillas & Perfect Roasted Veggies	Creamy Nutrient-Dense Ice Cream
Thursday	Vitamin C–Avocado Smoothie	Seafood Red Curry	Simplified Bone Broth	Beef Tongue Birria w/Fresh Corn Tortillas & Perfect Roasted Veggies	Grain-Free Chocolate Chip Cookies
Friday	Clean-the-Fridge Omelet	Beef Tongue Birria w/Fresh Corn Tortillas & Perfect Roasted Veggies	Simplified Bone Broth	Family-Size Pork Carnitas w/Fresh Corn Tortillas & Perfect Roasted Veggies	Creamy Nutrient-Dense Ice Cream
Saturday	Vitamin C–Avocado Smoothie	Finish leftovers from the week.		Finish leftovers from the week.	Grain-Free Chocolate Chip Cookies

Meal Prep Schedule

Starting Notes

- One day before your first meal prep day, add the spice rub to the Family-Size Pork Carnitas (page 55) and let it sit in the fridge.

- The carnitas and roasted veggies can be used in the Clean-the-Fridge Omelet (page 116). I recommend making the omelet fresh in the morning.

Meal Prep Day #1

- If you don't have bone broth on hand, start a batch of Simplified Bone Broth (page 30). Prepare the dough for the Fresh Corn Tortillas (page 77) and set it aside to let it rest for one hour.

- While the bone broth cooks, cook the Family-Size Pork Carnitas (page 55) in an oven-safe dish or slow cooker. Prepare the Perfect Roasted Veggies (page 83) and finish the Fresh Corn Tortillas (page 77).

- Portion out the ingredients for the Vitamin C–Avocado Smoothie (page 103).

- Prepare the Seafood Red Curry (page 59) for dinner and store the leftovers.

- Once the carnitas is fork-tender, store it. Make a batch of Creamy Nutrient-Dense Ice Cream (page 122) for the week.

Meal Prep Day #2

- In the beginning of the day on Tuesday, begin cooking the Beef Tongue Birria (page 49) in a pot over low heat or in a slow cooker.

- In the evening, finish the birria—serve it for dinner and store the leftovers.

- Make a batch of the Grain-Free Chocolate Chip Cookies (page 134). Serve for dessert and store the uncooked dough in the freezer.

Week 4

Breakfast #1: Savory Masa Bowl (page 107)

Breakfast #2: High-Protein Pancakes (page 115)

Protein #1: My Hearty Organ Meat Chili (page 41)

Protein #2: Easy Roasted Chicken (page 34)

Carb #1: Middle Eastern Lentil Salad (page 70)

Snack #1: 15-Minute Chicken Liver Mousse (page 29)

Dessert #1: Gluten-Free Fermented Banana Bread (page 133)

Dessert #2: Single-Serving Key Lime Pie (page 138)

Suggested Schedule

	Breakfast	Lunch	Snack (optional)	Dinner	Dessert (optional)
Sunday	Finish leftovers from the prior week.	Use up leftovers or go out to lunch!		Easy Roasted Chicken w/Middle Eastern Lentil Salad	Single-Serving Key Lime Pie
Monday	Savory Masa Bowl	Easy Roasted Chicken w/Middle Eastern Lentil Salad	15-Minute Chicken Liver Mousse	My Hearty Organ Meat Chili	Gluten-Free Fermented Banana Bread
Tuesday	High-Protein Pancakes	My Hearty Organ Meat Chili	Gluten-Free Fermented Banana Bread	Easy Roasted Chicken w/Middle Eastern Lentil Salad	Single-Serving Key Lime Pie
Wednesday	Savory Masa Bowl	My Hearty Organ Meat Chili	15-Minute Chicken Liver Mousse	Easy Roasted Chicken w/Middle Eastern Lentil Salad	Gluten-Free Fermented Banana Bread
Thursday	High-Protein Pancakes	Easy Roasted Chicken w/Middle Eastern Lentil Salad	Gluten-Free Fermented Banana Bread	My Hearty Organ Meat Chili	Single-Serving Key Lime Pie
Friday	Savory Masa Bowl	Easy Roasted Chicken w/Middle Eastern Lentil Salad	15-Minute Chicken Liver Mousse	My Hearty Organ Meat Chili	Gluten-Free Fermented Banana Bread
Saturday	High-Protein Pancakes	Finish leftovers from the week.		Finish leftovers from the week.	Single-Serving Key Lime Pie

Meal Prep Schedule

Starting Notes

- One day before your first meal prep day, generously salt the chicken and stick it back in the fridge. Start soaking the lentils for the Middle Eastern Lentil Salad (page 70).

Meal Prep Day #1

- Bring the chicken out of the fridge and let it come to room temperature for 1 hour.

- While the chicken sits out, prepare the 15-Minute Chicken Liver Mousse (page 29). Prepare three servings of the base of the Savory Masa Bowl (page 107) for breakfasts.

- Begin the fermentation process of the Gluten-Free Fermented Banana Bread (page 133) by combining the blended buckwheat and water and set it aside overnight.

- Prepare the Easy Roasted Chicken (page 34) and the Middle Eastern Lentil Salad (page 70). Serve for dinner and store the leftovers.

- Prepare the Single-Serving Key Lime Pie (page 138). Serve for dessert and store the leftovers.

Meal Prep Day #2

- Three hours before dinner on Monday, prepare My Hearty Organ Meat Chili (page 41).

- While the chili cooks, prepare the rest of the batter for the Gluten-Free Fermented Banana Bread (page 133). Also, prepare the High-Protein Pancakes (page 115)—you can cook them and store the pancakes in the fridge or keep the batter in the fridge and make them fresh at breakfast time throughout the week.

- Bake the banana bread while you eat the chili for dinner.

Week 5

Breakfast #1: Cottage Cheese Breakfast Parfait (page 112)

Breakfast #2: Breakfast Fried Rice (page 111)

Protein #1: Comforting Short Rib Ragu (page 46)

Protein #2: Nutrient-Rich Liver Meatballs (page 38)

Protein #3: Maple Salmon Bites (page 60)

Carb #1: Prebiotic Potato Salad (page 69)

Veggie #1: Simple Dill Carrot Salad (page 95)

Snack #1: Grain-Free Frosted Pumpkin Bread (page 130)

Dessert #1: Grain-Free Chocolate Chip Cookies (page 134)

Suggested Schedule

	Breakfast	Lunch	Snack (optional)	Dinner	Dessert (optional)
Sunday	Finish leftovers from the prior week.	Use up leftovers or go out to lunch!		Nutrient-Rich Liver Meatballs w/ Prebiotic Potato Salad	Grain-Free Frosted Pumpkin Bread
Monday	Cottage Cheese Breakfast Parfait	Nutrient-Rich Liver Meatballs w/ Prebiotic Potato Salad	Grain-Free Frosted Pumpkin Bread	Comforting Short Rib Ragu	Grain-Free Chocolate Chip Cookies
Tuesday	Breakfast Fried Rice	Nutrient-Rich Liver Meatballs w/ Prebiotic Potato Salad	Cottage Cheese Breakfast Parfait	Maple Salmon Bites w/ Simple Dill Carrot Salad	Grain-Free Frosted Pumpkin Bread
Wednesday	Cottage Cheese Breakfast Parfait	Comforting Short Rib Ragu	Grain-Free Frosted Pumpkin Bread	Maple Salmon Bites w/ Simple Dill Carrot Salad	Grain-Free Chocolate Chip Cookies
Thursday	Breakfast Fried Rice	Maple Salmon Bites w/ Simple Dill Carrot Salad	Cottage Cheese Breakfast Parfait	Comforting Short Rib Ragu	Grain-Free Frosted Pumpkin Bread
Friday	Cottage Cheese Breakfast Parfait	Comforting Short Rib Ragu	Grain-Free Frosted Pumpkin Bread	Nutrient-Rich Liver Meatballs w/ Prebiotic Potato Salad	Grain-Free Chocolate Chip Cookies
Saturday	Breakfast Fried Rice	Finish leftovers from the week.		Finish leftovers from the week.	Finish leftovers from the week.

Meal Prep Schedule

Meal Prep Day #1

- Start by preparing the Comforting Short Rib Ragu (page 46).

- While the ragu cooks, prepare the Cottage Cheese Breakfast Parfaits (page 112) and the Prebiotic Potato Salad (page 69). Prepare the Grain-Free Frosted Pumpkin Bread (page 130) batter and set aside. Prepare the Nutrient-Rich Liver Meatballs (page 38) and brown them in the pan, then set aside.

- Once the ragu is done, increase the oven temperature to 350°F (180°C) to finish cooking the meatballs and bake the bread.

Meal Prep Day #2

- On Tuesday evening, prepare the Maple Salmon Bites (page 60) and the Simple Dill Carrot Salad (page 95). Serve for dinner and store the leftovers.

- Prepare a batch of the Grain-Free Chocolate Chip Cookies (page 134). You can bake them all and store in the fridge or bake enough for dessert and then store the dough balls in the freezer to bake fresh throughout the rest of the week.

Easy-Prep Proteins

Quality protein is an essential part of your plate. Your body relies on the amino acids in protein for many essential tasks, such as building muscles and bones, repairing tissue, regulating hormones and making enzymes. Many people struggle to get enough protein in their day, which can lead to blood sugar spikes, cravings, hormone imbalances and more. Having meat prepped and ready to go is the best way to ensure you will create balanced meals throughout the week. In this chapter, you will find recipes for a range of animal proteins, which provide the most bioavailable protein—meaning the protein that our bodies can best absorb and utilize. My Easy Roasted Chicken (page 34) is one of my favorites—it is so simple and delicious and makes a big batch of meat that you can use in a variety of ways throughout the week. The Nutrient-Rich Liver Meatballs (page 38) are packed with flavors and are a great way to incorporate beef liver into your diet.

15-Minute Chicken Liver Mousse

Liver is one of the most nutrient-dense foods available. It's rich in iron, vitamins A and B$_{12}$ and copper, making it great for boundless energy and glowing skin. A common misconception is that livers store all of the toxins, so we wouldn't want to eat that. Actually, the liver's role is to filter toxins to be excreted from the body—it's a processer of toxins, not a storage area. Check out the sourcing tips at the beginning of the book for finding quality organ meat (page 9). If you don't love the taste of liver—even in this decadent mousse—don't worry; I have a few recipes where you can hide the liver within other meat and get all of the nutrients without any of the flavor—check out the Nutrient-Rich Liver Meatballs (page 38) and My Hearty Organ Meat Chili (page 41).

Yield: 24 servings

---

1 lb (455 g) fresh chicken livers

¾ cup (171 g/1½ sticks) grass-fed salted butter, cut into cubes and divided

2 medium-sized shallots, peeled and diced

1 tbsp (3 g) fresh thyme leaves, chopped

⅓ cup (80 ml) port or Simplified Bone Broth (page 30)

3 tbsp (45 ml) organic heavy cream, plus more as needed

Sea salt (optional)

Start by trimming the livers of any connective tissue—the white, stringy bits. Set aside the trimmed liver.

In a large skillet, melt 4 tablespoons (57 g) of the butter over medium heat. Add the shallots and sauté until fragrant, about 3 minutes.

Add the trimmed livers, thyme and port. Cook over medium heat for approximately 5 minutes, occasionally stirring the livers, until the wine has reduced. The livers should be browned but very soft and pink on the inside.

Remove the pan from the heat, and transfer the mixture into a blender or food processor with the cream and 4 more tablespoons (57 g) of butter. Puree until smooth, adding a little more cream if necessary. Taste and adjust the seasoning, adding salt if necessary.

Pack the mousse into glass jars or ramekins, then smooth the top with a spatula. Melt the remaining 4 tablespoons (57 g) of butter and pour a thin layer of melted butter over each dish. Cover and refrigerate until firm before enjoying, about 2 hours.

If the mousse is covered with a thin layer of butter, it can be kept in the fridge for up to a month. Each time you dig into the mousse and break the seal, reseal with butter to preserve it.

To freeze, store in an airtight container for up to 3 months. When you're ready to enjoy, thaw the mousse in the fridge overnight.

Simplified Bone Broth

Bone broth is a staple in my kitchen. I always have a batch in my fridge, plus some backup stored in my freezer. It's a versatile cooking ingredient that can make veggies delicious, is perfect for braising meat and is a go-to base for soups, but it also packs impressive health benefits. Bone broth is rich in gelatin, which can support a healthy gut lining. Plus, since bone broth is made by simmering the bones and connective tissue of animals, it's a great way to reduce waste and use the whole animal! Whenever you cook a full bird or other bone-in meat, save the bones in a freezer bag and use them to make bone broth. You can also save veggie scraps such as onion peels, celery pieces and carrot tops to add to your broth.

Yield: 18 cups (4.3 L)

---

4 lb (1.8 kg) beef knuckle bones

2 lb (905 g) chicken feet and/or backs

2 cups (260 g) veggie scraps (onion, garlic, celery, carrots) (optional)

Cold filtered water

1 tbsp (15 ml) apple cider vinegar (optional)

1 tbsp (18 g) sea salt

In a large stockpot, combine the bones and veggies (if using). Fill the pot with just enough filtered water to barely cover the bones. You can add a splash of apple cider vinegar if you want, then let it sit for 30 minutes. It is thought that the acid from vinegar can help draw out nutrients from the bones.

Add the sea salt, bring the pot to a boil, then lower the heat to medium.

Cover the pot with a lid and cook at a rolling simmer—you will see lots of bubbles popping up—for 7 to 10 hours. During the first hour of cooking, I recommend skimming and discarding the foam and impurities that rise to the top. Do not stir the broth; stirring will make it cloudy.

Remove the broth from the heat and let it chill until cool enough to handle. Strain the broth through a fine-mesh sieve into glass storage containers.

Store in the fridge for 7 to 10 days, or in the freezer for 4 to 6 months. If you are storing in glass, leave 3 to 4 inches (8 to 10 cm) of headspace in the jar and ensure the broth is cooled completely before freezing.

You can repeat the process with the bones one more time to make another batch.

Turmeric Pickled Eggs

These pickled eggs are a great way to extend the shelf life of eggs and stock your fridge with easy-to-use, nutrient-packed eggs. Eggs are a powerhouse of nutrients, containing quality protein, healthy fats and such essential nutrients as choline, folate and selenium. This makes them great for brain health, energy production and good immune function. Eat these straight out of the jar for a nutrient-rich snack or slice them up and toss on toasts, salads, soups or curries for a tangy addition. They also turn a beautiful yellow color, and everyone knows colorful eggs are more fun to eat! You can try out different spices for different flavor profiles.

Yield: 12 eggs

1 cup (240 ml) apple cider vinegar

1 cup (240 ml) water

1 tbsp (6 g) curry powder

1 tsp ground turmeric

¼ tsp sea salt

1 tsp raw honey (optional)

12 large hard-boiled eggs

3 cloves garlic

In a saucepan, combine the apple cider vinegar, water, curry powder, turmeric, sea salt and honey (if using). Heat over low heat for 5 minutes until dissolved and combined, then remove from the heat.

In a large jar, combine the eggs and garlic, then cover with the liquid. Transfer to the fridge and refrigerate for 2 to 3 days before serving.

Store in the refrigerator for 3 to 4 months.

Easy Roasted Chicken

Here's a staple recipe that everyone should have in their nutrient-dense arsenal. I always recommend that people opt for a whole chicken over individual cuts of chicken—you will get way more meat and nutrition for the price, and it's a great meal prep for your week. Roasting a whole chicken can seem daunting and then be a letdown when it comes out dry and flavorless. But I have a secret weapon for you—when you salt the chicken 24 hours in advance, the salt breaks down the proteins in the chicken, leaving a moist, tender and flavorful bird every time.

Remember to save the chicken carcass and use it for broth!

Yield: 6 servings

1 (4- to 6-lb [1.8- to 2.7-kg]) chicken

Sea salt

3 tbsp (54 g) salted butter, at room temperature

1 tbsp (8 g) za'atar seasoning

1 lemon, cut into slices, divided

1 onion, quartered, divided

1 head garlic, cut in half crosswise

1 tbsp (15 ml) extra virgin olive oil

Twenty-four hours before you plan on cooking, remove the chicken from the fridge, remove the giblets and salt the chicken liberally all over, including inside the cavity. Return it to the fridge.

On the day of cooking, remove the chicken from the fridge 1 hour before cooking to let it come to room temperature, and preheat the oven to 425°F (220°C).

In a small bowl, combine the butter with the za'atar seasoning. Smother the chicken all over with the butter mixture. Stuff half of the lemon slices and onion into the cavity of the chicken.

In a roasting pan or cast-iron skillet, scatter the remaining onion and lemon, along with the garlic, and cover with the olive oil. Arrange the garlic so that it is cut side down on the pan. Place the chicken on top.

Roast for 20 minutes, then lower the temperature to 400°F (200°C) and continue to roast for another 40 minutes, or until the chicken is cooked through (it should have an internal temperature of 165°F [73°C] and the juices should run clear when you cut between the leg and thigh).

Remove the chicken from the oven and let cool for 10 minutes, then carve it. Serve it with the roasted onion and garlic and the drippings in the pan.

To freeze, butcher the chicken by removing each leg and thigh, then each wing and finally each breast. You can then cut the meat to your liking and store in an airtight container in the freezer for up to 6 months. To reheat, let it thaw in the fridge and reheat in a hot skillet.

Simple Curry Chicken Salad

Chicken salad is a great meal prep item because it comes together with a few simple ingredients. This version uses my 5-Ingredient Mayonnaise (page 143) to ensure it's packed with healthy fats and tastes fresh. Use the chicken breast from the Easy Roasted Chicken (page 34) or boil a few chicken breasts in water until cooked, and you have the easiest meal prep protein that you can add to a piece of toast or salad to keep you fueled all week long.

Yield: 6 servings

3 cups (420 g) chopped cooked chicken breast

3 celery ribs, diced

1 green onion, sliced finely

½ cup (115 g) 5-Ingredient Mayonnaise (page 143), or more as needed

1 tsp curry powder

½ tsp smoked paprika

Sea salt and freshly ground black pepper

In a large bowl, combine the chicken, celery, green onion and mayonnaise, and stir together. The mayonnaise should moisten the chicken—add more or less as preferred.

Stir in the curry powder and smoked paprika. Taste and adjust the seasoning to your liking and add salt and pepper as needed. You can experiment with additional mix-ins, such as apples, nuts, raisins and other veggies.

Store in the fridge for 4 to 5 days.

Nutrient-Rich Liver Meatballs

Everyone loves meatballs! They are the perfect meal prep protein because they can be made in large batches, they freeze well and they are so versatile that you'll never get sick of them. Your standard meatball is a great nutrient-dense meal, but the added liver makes these meatballs a nutrient powerhouse full of iron, zinc and B vitamins to give you a boost of natural energy. This recipe is perfect if you are hesitant about liver but still want the benefits because you can't taste it at all when it's mixed with the other meat and spices.

Yield: 8 to 10 servings

1 lb (455 g) ground beef

1 lb (455 g) ground pork

2 to 4 oz (55 to 115 g) beef or chicken liver, grated finely or minced

1 large egg

2 tsp (12 g) sea salt

1 tsp dried oregano

½ tsp red pepper flakes

½ tsp onion powder

½ tsp garlic powder

1 tbsp (14 g) beef tallow or ghee

Preheat your oven to 350°F (180°C).

In a large bowl, combine the beef, pork, liver, egg, salt, oregano, red pepper flakes, onion powder and garlic powder, and mix until combined. Shape the mixture into meatballs slightly larger than golf balls.

Heat an oven-safe skillet over medium heat and add the beef tallow. Add the meatballs to the pan, working in batches if necessary to not overcrowd the pan, and brown them for 2 to 3 minutes on each side.

Once all the meatballs are browned, add all of them back to the pan, transfer the dish to the oven and cook until the meat is cooked through, 5 to 8 minutes.

Serve with Gut-Friendly Herb Rice (page 74), Middle Eastern Lentil Salad (page 70) or Bone Broth Braised Greens (page 88) for a delicious, balanced meal.

Store in the fridge in an airtight container for 4 to 5 days, or freeze for 3 to 4 months. To reheat, let the meatballs thaw in the fridge and reheat in a 350°F (180°C) oven or in a hot skillet on the stovetop until warmed through.

My Hearty Organ Meat Chili

This is the most nutrient-dense, delicious chili you will ever make! It's loaded with bioavailable essential nutrients, including vitamin A, B vitamins, copper and iron from the beef heart and liver. Organ meat chili is the best way to serve picky eaters or those who are not a fan of organ meat because the spices mask the flavor completely. It also freezes great, so make a big batch and serve it for a few meals, then stock your freezer with comforting chili for a day that you run out of groceries or don't feel like cooking!

Yield: 10 servings

---

1 lb (455 g) beef stew meat

Sea salt

3 tsp (14 g) beef tallow or ghee, divided

½ yellow onion, diced

3 cloves garlic, minced

1 lb (455 g) ground beef

2 oz (55 g) beef liver, grated finely or minced

2 oz (55 g) beef heart, grated finely or minced

1 (28-oz [800-g]) can chopped tomatoes

½ cup (120 ml) Simplified Bone Broth (page 30)

1½ tbsp (11 g) chili powder

1 tbsp (6 g) unsweetened raw cacao powder

½ tsp cayenne pepper (optional)

2 medium-sized zucchini, chopped

1 medium-sized sweet potato, chopped

Optional Toppings
Fresh cilantro

Sliced green onions

Sour cream

Pitted, peeled and sliced avocado

Shredded Cheddar cheese

Preheat the oven to 300°F (150°C).

Generously season the stew meat with sea salt on all sides. In a large, oven-safe pot over medium-high heat, heat 1½ teaspoons (7 g) of the beef tallow and brown the stew meat for 2 minutes on each side.

Remove the meat from the pan and lower the heat to medium. Add the remaining 1½ teaspoons (7 g) of tallow. Add the onion and garlic, and sauté until fragrant, 3 to 4 minutes. Use a wooden spoon to scrape up any brown bits from the pan.

Add the ground beef to the pot. Use a wooden spoon to break up the meat and cook until browned and almost fully cooked. Stir in the beef liver and beef heart. Add the stew meat back into the pot and stir to combine.

Stir in the canned tomatoes and bone broth. Season with chili powder, cacao powder, cayenne (if using) and ¼ teaspoon of salt. Stir to combine. Place a lid on the pot and transfer to the oven. Cook for 2 hours.

After 2 hours, stir in the zucchini and sweet potato. Cover, return the pot to the oven and cook for 1 more hour. The meat should be fork-tender. Serve with cilantro, green onions, sour cream, avocado, Cheddar cheese or whatever other toppings you like!

Store in an airtight container in the fridge for 4 to 5 days. To freeze, divide into desired portion sizes and freeze for 3 to 4 months. To reheat, thaw the chili in the fridge overnight and warm in a saucepan over medium heat until warmed through.

Thai Larb Lettuce Cups

This is a great dish for a hands-on dinner party or for meal prep, since it makes a large serving of protein. You can whip up this delicious, Thai-inspired dish in just 20 minutes and serve it with a variety of toppings, such as fresh herbs, green onions, pickled onions and chopped nuts. Each person can assemble their lettuce wraps with their personalized toppings! The meat is served in lettuce cups for a low-carb, grain-free meal, but you can also use the meat throughout the week in rice bowls to switch up your meals.

Yield: 8 to 10 servings

1 tbsp (14 g) beef tallow, divided

1 onion, diced

3 cloves garlic, minced

2 carrots, diced

1 Thai chile pepper, diced (optional)

8 oz (225 g) shiitake mushrooms, diced

1 lb (455 g) ground pork

1 lb (455 g) ground beef

1 (3" [8-cm]) piece fresh ginger, peeled

1 tsp red pepper flakes

2½ tbsp (38 ml) tamari or coconut aminos

1 tsp fish sauce

Juice of 1 lime

For Serving

Toasted sesame oil

Sesame seeds

Bibb lettuce cups

Optional toppings, such as fresh mint, green onions, pickled onions, sliced cucumbers and lacto-fermented carrots

In a large skillet, heat 1½ teaspoons (7 g) of the tallow over medium heat. Add the onion, garlic, carrots and chile pepper (if using) to the pan. Stir and cook for 2 to 3 minutes.

Add the mushrooms and cook for another 5 to 6 minutes, stirring occasionally, until they cook down. Transfer the mixture to a large bowl and set aside.

Add the remaining 1½ teaspoons (7 g) of tallow to the pan. Add the ground pork and use a wooden spoon to crumble the meat, and cook until browned and mostly cooked through, 6 to 8 minutes. Drain any liquid from the pan and transfer the meat to the bowl containing the onion mixture.

Add the ground beef to the pan. Break up the meat with a wooden spoon, and cook until browned and mostly cooked through, 6 to 8 minutes. Drain any liquid from the pan.

Return the ground pork and onion mixture to the pan that contains the beef and stir to combine. Grate the ginger directly into the pot and add the red pepper flakes. Cook for another 1 to 2 minutes.

Remove the pan from the heat and stir in the tamari and fish sauce. Stir in the lime juice. Taste and adjust the seasoning if needed.

Drizzle with toasted sesame oil and sesame seeds before serving. Serve with lettuce cups and fresh mint, green onions, pickled onions, sliced cucumbers, fermented carrots and any other topping you like!

Store in the fridge for 4 to 5 days. To freeze, store in freezer containers in desired portion sizes for up to 3 months. To reheat, let thaw in the fridge and heat over medium heat in a saucepan until warmed through.

Nourishing Beef Heart Jerky

No one will know that this delicious beef jerky is actually organ meat! This is one of my favorite ways to add organ meat to my family's diet. It is salty and sweet like your typical beef jerky but with some additional micronutrients, including iron, selenium, zinc and B vitamins, which support good energy levels. This is a terrific high-protein snack to pack in lunches, bring with you when you travel or eat on the go. Beef heart works great for jerky because it's a lean cut of meat. Plus, organs like beef heart are typically more affordable than more common muscle meats, so you can make some budget-friendly, nose-to-tail jerky.

Yield: 6 servings

2 lb (905 g) beef heart or London broil, sliced thinly

1 orange, peeled

⅓ cup (80 ml) apple cider vinegar

⅓ cup (80 ml) organic tamari or coconut aminos

1½ tsp (9 g) sea salt (omit if using tamari)

2 tbsp (30 ml) raw honey

5 cloves garlic, peeled and roughly chopped

3 tbsp (15 g) fresh ginger, peeled and roughly chopped

1 tbsp (4 g) red pepper flakes

Trim away any excess fat from the beef heart, then slice it as thinly as possible. My trick for thinly slicing meat is to work with a semifrozen cut of the meat. Start slicing the beef heart before it is thawed completely or place it in the freezer for 30 minutes before you begin to slice.

To make the marinade, in a blender, combine the orange, apple cider vinegar, organic tamari, salt (if using), honey, garlic, ginger and red pepper flakes, and blend until well mixed.

Place the sliced meat in a glass container and cover with the marinade. Mix until most or all of the meat is submerged in the marinade. Cover and let sit in the fridge for 24 to 48 hours, shaking the container a few times during that time to ensure the meat is equally marinated.

Once the meat is done marinating, remove it from the marinade and wipe off any excess liquid.

To cook in a dehydrator, place the meat in a single layer on dehydrator sheets and cook on the jerky setting (around 150°F [66°C]) for 6 to 8 hours.

To dry it in the oven, place the meat in a single layer on a baking sheet fitted with a rack and bake at 170°F (77°C)—or the lowest setting of your oven—until dry, 4 to 5 hours.

Store in an airtight container in your pantry for up to 1 week or in your fridge for up to 2 weeks.

Comforting Short Rib Ragu

Braising larger, bone-in cuts of meat, such as short ribs, is a foolproof way to get tender, fall-off-the-bone meat. This is my go-to dish when I want to impress a crowd or treat a loved one to a deliciously rich and comforting meal—it's an easy meal with impressive results. It's great for meal prep because it only gets tastier as it sits in the fridge, and you can pair it with so many things—pasta, rice, polenta, veggies—so you will never get tired of it. Plus, most of the cooking time is hands-off, letting the short ribs braise, so this is a supersimple dish that only takes about 20 minutes of your attention and effort.

Yield: 8 to 10 servings

3 lb (1.4 kg) bone-in beef short ribs

Sea salt

1 tbsp (14 g) beef tallow

1 yellow onion, diced

4 cloves garlic, minced

3 large carrots, diced

3 celery ribs, diced

3 tbsp (48 g) tomato paste

1 cup (240 ml) dry red wine (e.g., cabernet sauvignon) or Simplified Bone Broth (page 30)

1 cup (240 ml) Simplified Bone Broth (page 30)

1 (14-oz [400-g]) can crushed tomatoes

1 tbsp (2 g) fresh rosemary, chopped finely

1½ tsp (1 g) fresh thyme, chopped finely

Twenty-four hours before cooking, liberally season the meat on all sides with salt and return it to the fridge.

One to two hours before you cook, let the short ribs sit on the counter to come to room temperature.

Preheat the oven to 325°F (170°C).

Heat a large oven-safe pot, such as a Dutch oven, over medium-high heat and add the tallow. Add the meat to the pan and sear on all sides until browned, about 3 minutes per side. Remove the meat from the pot and set aside.

Add the onion, garlic, carrots and celery to the same pot and sauté until fragrant, 2 to 3 minutes.

Add the tomato paste to the pot and stir. Add the red wine to deglaze the pan, using a wooden spoon to scrape up any brown bits off the bottom of the pan, and let simmer for 5 to 8 minutes.

Return the meat to the pot and add the broth and the crushed tomatoes to cover the meat. Add the rosemary and thyme. Put on the lid and transfer to the oven to cook for 3 to 4 hours, or until the meat is fork-tender.

This can also be cooked in a slow cooker or Instant Pot®. To cook in a slow cooker, transfer the browned meat and veggies into a slow cooker and cook on LOW for 8 hours or HIGH for 6 hours.

(continued)

Comforting Short Rib Ragu (continued)

Once the meat is tender and falling off the bone, transfer the meat to a cutting board. Use a fork to separate the meat from the bones and shred it. Discard the bones, return the meat to the sauce and stir to combine.

Serve over pasta, over the Gut-Friendly Herb Rice (page 74) or with the Cheesy Scalloped Potatoes (page 66) alongside the Perfect Roasted Veggies (page 83).

Store in an airtight container in the fridge for 4 to 5 days. To freeze, divide into desired portion sizes and freeze in airtight containers for 3 to 4 months. To reheat, thaw overnight in the fridge and reheat in a skillet until cooked through.

Beef Tongue Birria

This recipe is inspired by birria de res—*a Mexican beef stew that is also used to make the popular* quesabirria *tacos. Preparing the beef tongue in a birria style produces a flavorful and tender meat with a delicious broth. While it is an organ meat, when cooked correctly—braised until fork-tender—beef tongue is a tender cut of meat with mild flavor similar to more common muscle meat. It is rich in healthy fats that give it a soft, melt-in-your-mouth texture and provide significant health benefits. Beef tongue is rich in iron and zinc, which supports immune function, provides choline and vitamin B_{12} for improved brain health and is a source of complete protein. You can serve the meat in the broth as a soup or turn the meat into cheesy tacos, using the Fresh Corn Tortillas (page 77), and serve it with a bowl of consommé.*

Yield: 6 servings

1 beef tongue

1 qt (946 ml) Simplified Bone Broth (page 30)

1 onion, quartered, divided

2 bay leaves

1½ tsp (9 g) sea salt

3 dried ancho chiles, seeded

5 dried guajillo chiles, seeded

1 tbsp (15 ml) extra virgin olive oil

5 cloves garlic, chopped roughly

2 small tomatoes, quartered

1 tbsp (15 ml) apple cider vinegar

½ tsp ground cumin

Freshly ground black pepper

Fresh cilantro, diced white onion and lime wedges, for serving

In a large pot, combine the beef tongue, bone broth, half of the onion, the bay leaves and sea salt. Add water as needed to fully cover the tongue. Cover the pot with a lid and bring to a boil, then lower the heat and let simmer for 30 minutes.

While the tongue simmers, heat a medium skillet over medium-high heat for 2 to 3 minutes. Add the ancho and guajillo chiles to the pan and lightly toast them, about 1 to 2 minutes per side, being careful not to burn them. Transfer the toasted chiles to a heat-safe bowl and cover with hot water. Let them sit for 8 to 10 minutes to rehydrate.

Over medium heat, reheat the skillet that had been used for the chiles and add the olive oil. Add the remaining half of the onion and the garlic to the pan and sauté until fragrant, 2 to 3 minutes. Add the tomatoes and cook for another 4 to 5 minutes. Remove from the heat.

Drain the rehydrated chiles. In a blender or food processer, combine the rehydrated chiles, sautéed onion, garlic, tomatoes, apple cider vinegar, cumin and a few cracks of black pepper. Add a cup (240 ml) of broth from the pot that contains the tongue. Blend until smooth.

(continued)

Beef Tongue Birria (continued)

Use a fine-mesh sieve to strain the mixture into the pot containing the tongue. Cover the pot and let simmer until the tongue is fork-tender, about 4 hours on the stovetop. Alternatively, transfer the entire mixture to a slow cooker and cook on HIGH for 6 hours.

Once the tongue is tender, remove it from the broth and let it cool. Use your hands to peel off the outer layer of the tongue. It should come off easily, or you can use a knife to make a shallow cut into the tongue to start the peeling process. Discard the outer layer. Chop the tongue into small cubes and return it to the broth to serve as a soup with fresh cilantro, diced white onion and a wedge of lime.

To make quesabirria tacos, remove the meat from the broth. Dip a corn tortilla into the broth and place in a hot skillet. Fill with cheese and meat, then fold in half into a quesadilla. Serve the quesabirria with a strained cup of the cooking broth on the side, with cilantro and onion.

Store in an airtight container in the fridge for 4 to 5 days. To freeze, divide into desired portion sizes and store in an airtight container for up to 3 months. To reheat, let thaw in the fridge overnight and heat in a saucepan until warmed through.

Make-and-Freeze Kebabs

These flavorful kebabs are going to be your family's new weekly staple—and it's a bonus that it has beef liver that no one will taste! The mixture of beef, lamb, cheese and spices results in a juicy protein to have on hand. Make these at the start of the week and serve them for breakfast, lunch or dinner with salad, a side of veggies, rice bowls or wraps. The options are endless, so make sure you always have a batch in your freezer! Serve these with the Spicy Cilantro Sauce (page 147) for a mind-blowing flavor combination.

Yield: 8 to 10 servings

1 lb (455 g) ground beef

1 lb (455 g) ground lamb

2 oz (55 g) beef liver, grated or minced finely

1 cup (120 g) shredded Cheddar cheese

1 tbsp (5 g) grated fresh ginger

2 tsp (12 g) sea salt

2 tsp (4 g) curry powder

1½ tbsp (11 g) chili powder

½ tsp za'atar seasoning

Spicy Cilantro Sauce (page 147), for serving

Preheat the oven to 350°F (180°C).

In a large bowl, combine the ground beef, ground lamb, beef liver, Cheddar cheese, ginger, sea salt, curry powder, chili powder and za'atar seasoning, and mix well.

Use your hands to form ½ cup (120 g) of the meat mixture into a kebab shape (small log) and transfer to a baking sheet. Continue until all the kebabs are formed.

Bake for 25 to 30 minutes, until they are cooked through and the inside is no longer pink.

If you prefer to grill them, form the meat into kebabs on skewers and let them firm up in the fridge for 4 hours or overnight before grilling. Heat the grill to high heat and cook for 12 to 15 minutes, or until cooked through, turning halfway through.

Serve with the Spicy Cilantro Sauce (page 147) and the Middle Eastern Lentil Salad (page 70).

Store in an airtight container in the fridge for 4 to 5 days. Freeze in an airtight container for 3 to 4 months. To reheat, let thaw in the fridge overnight and heat in a 350°F (180°C) oven until warmed through.

Family-Size Pork Carnitas

Taco night just got more delicious and even more time friendly. Slow cooking a pork shoulder requires only a few minutes of hands-on effort and yields a huge batch of tender, flavorful meat. Prep a batch of this carnitas meat to serve a large crowd or stock your fridge to feed a family all week. Not only is this dish a great source of quality protein, but pork is rich in such essential nutrients as thiamine, vitamins B_6 and B_{12}, selenium and zinc.

Yield: 9 to 10 servings

1 tbsp (15 ml) extra virgin olive oil

1 tbsp (18 g) sea salt

1 tbsp (2 g) dried oregano

1½ tsp (4 g) ground cumin

1 tsp smoked paprika

1 (5- to 6-lb [2.3- to 2.7-kg]) bone-in pork shoulder

1 yellow onion, diced

1 jalapeño pepper, seeded and chopped

5 cloves garlic, minced

1 cup (240 ml) fresh orange juice

1 cup (240 ml) Simplified Bone Broth (page 30)

Twenty-four to 48 hours before you will be cooking the meat, make the marinade: In a small bowl, combine the olive oil, sea salt, oregano, cumin and smoked paprika. Massage the marinade into the pork shoulder and return it to the fridge to marinate for 24 to 48 hours.

On the day of cooking, remove the meat from the fridge and let it come to room temperature for 1 to 2 hours before cooking.

This can be cooked in an oven or a pressure cooker. If you're baking it, preheat the oven to 275°F (140°C).

In a large, oven-safe dish, combine the meat, onion, jalapeño, garlic, orange juice and bone broth. Bake for 4 hours, or until the meat is fork-tender. Alternatively, cook the mixture in your slow cooker on the LOW setting for 8 hours or on the HIGH setting for 6 hours.

Once the pork is cooked through and fork-tender, use a fork to shred the meat, reserving the cooking juices. When you are ready to serve, on a baking sheet, combine the shredded meat with 1 cup (240 ml) of its cooking juices, and broil for 2 to 3 minutes, or until crispy.

Serve with Fresh Corn Tortillas (page 77) or in a bowl with the Gut-Friendly Herb Rice (page 74). I love to top it with white onion, fresh cilantro, radish and the Probiotic-Rich Salsa (page 144) or Fermented Hot Sauce (page 161).

You can store this in the fridge for 4 days or in the freezer for up to 6 months. To reheat, thaw in the fridge overnight and bake in a 350°F (180°C) oven until warmed through. Finish under the broiler for 1 to 2 minutes until crispy.

Batched Shepherd's Pie

My dad made the best shepherd's and cottage pies when I was growing up. To this day, this pie is one of my favorite meals to batch cook. It's comforting and satiating without being overly filling. You get quality protein from the meat mixture with some whole food carbohydrates in the potato topping. Plus, it makes a big batch so you can freeze into individual portions or two or three servings.

Yield: 10 servings

Filling
1 tbsp (15 ml) extra virgin olive oil

1 yellow onion, chopped

4 cloves garlic, minced

3 large carrots, medium diced

4 celery ribs, medium diced

Sea salt

2 lb (905 g) ground beef or ground lamb (see note)

1 tsp dried rosemary leaves

1 tsp dried thyme leaves

1 tbsp (15 ml) tamari

2 tbsp (16 g) tapioca flour

1½ tbsp (24 g) tomato paste

¾ cup (175 ml) Simplified Bone Broth (page 30)

½ cup (58 g) shredded Cheddar cheese

Potatoes
5 medium-sized Yukon Gold potatoes, cut into 1" (2.5-cm) cubes

Sea salt

¼ cup (57 g/½ stick) salted butter

¼ cup (60 ml) heavy cream

Note: You can use 2 pounds (905 g) of ground lamb or use a mixture of lamb and beef.

Make the filling: Heat a large, oven-safe skillet over medium-high heat and add the oil. Add the onion, garlic, carrots and celery, and cook for 5 minutes, stirring occasionally. Season with ¼ teaspoon of sea salt.

Add the ground beef to the skillet and break it apart with a wooden spoon. Cook for 6 to 8 minutes, or until the meat is browned, stirring occasionally.

Add the rosemary, thyme and tamari. Stir well. Sprinkle the tapioca flour over the meat, stirring to combine well so there are no clumps. Stir in the tomato paste until well incorporated and no clumps remain.

Stir in the bone broth and let it simmer for 8 to 10 minutes, stirring occasionally. Remove from the heat and preheat the oven to 350°F (180°C).

Make the potatoes: Place the potatoes in a large pot and cover with cold water. Add 1½ teaspoons (9 g) of sea salt to the water and bring to a boil. Lower the heat to a rolling simmer and cook for 8 to 10 minutes, or until the potatoes are fork-tender. Drain the potatoes, reserving 3 tablespoons (45 ml) of the cooking water. Mash the potatoes with the reserved cooking water, butter, heavy cream and a large pinch of sea salt just until they are creamy and all of their ingredients are well incorporated. Taste and add more salt as needed.

Cover the meat with an even layer of the mashed potatoes. Bake, uncovered, for 25 minutes. Then, add the cheese and bake for another 5 minutes, or until the cheese is melted. Broil for 1 to 2 minutes for a brown crust. Remove from the oven and let cool for 15 minutes before serving.

Store in an airtight container in the fridge for 4 to 5 days, or freeze in desired portion sizes for up to 3 months. To reheat, let thaw in the fridge overnight and heat in a 350°F (180°C) oven until warmed through.

Seafood Red Curry

This easy curry recipe is like takeout with added nutrients and less added sugar, at a fraction of the cost. It's also quicker—this dish comes together in 20 minutes and one pot. Shrimp is a great source of protein but also provides healthy omega-3 fatty acids that support heart health, as well as an impressive amount of minerals such as zinc, magnesium, iodine and phosphorus, making it a great nutrient-dense option.

Yield: 4 to 5 servings

1½ tsp (21 g) ghee

½ onion, diced

3 cloves garlic, minced

4 to 6 tsp (20 to 30 ml) red curry paste (see note)

3 cups (710 ml) Simplified Bone Broth (page 30)

1 large head broccoli, chopped

1 (13.5-oz [400-ml]) can coconut milk

1 tsp fish sauce

1 lb (455 g) wild shrimp

Fresh cilantro and lime wedges, for serving

Heat a large pot over medium-high heat and add the ghee. Add the onion, garlic and red curry paste. Cook for 2 minutes, stirring continuously.

Add the bone broth and stir to dissolve the paste. Simmer for 3 to 4 minutes. Add the broccoli and cook for another 3 minutes. Then, add the coconut milk and fish sauce.

Stir in the shrimp and let cook for 3 to 4 minutes until the shrimp is pink and cooked through and the broccoli is tender. Taste and adjust seasonings as needed. Serve over the Gut-Friendly Herb Rice (page 74) and garnish with fresh cilantro and a squeeze of lime juice.

Store in the fridge in airtight containers for 4 to 5 days, or freeze in desired portion sizes for 3 to 4 months. To reheat, let thaw in the fridge and heat in a saucepan over medium heat until warmed through.

Note: The spice level will vary based on the curry paste you use. Depending on your spice preferences, I recommend starting with 4 teaspoons (20 g) and adding more as needed.

Maple Salmon Bites

Fish is a bit challenging to meal prep, since its best cooked and eaten fresh, but we don't want to miss out on the amazing, healthy omega-3 fats from wild salmon. So, I made this super simple recipe that comes together in just 15 minutes for a nourishing meal to support healthy skin and promote brain and heart health. Plus, if you have leftovers, this dish works great the next day right out of the fridge—no stinky reheated fish here! Make an easy sushi bowl or roll with the toppings of your choice, such as green onion, avocado, seaweed, cucumber and carrot.

Yield: 3 to 4 servings

½ tsp Dijon mustard

2 tbsp (30 ml) pure maple syrup

2 tbsp (30 ml) tamari or coconut aminos

¼ tsp red pepper flakes

1 (2" [5-cm]) piece peeled fresh ginger

3 cloves garlic, peeled

1 lb (455 g) wild salmon, cut into 2" (5-cm) cubes

1 tsp smoked paprika

1½ tbsp (21 g) ghee, divided

Preheat the oven to 275°F (140°C).

Make the sauce: In a small bowl, combine the Dijon mustard, maple syrup, tamari and red pepper flakes. Grate the ginger and garlic directly into the bowl. Stir well to combine.

Place the salmon in a large bowl. Sprinkle the smoked paprika on the fish and massage until coated.

Heat a large oven-safe skillet over medium-high heat. Add 1 tablespoon (14 g) of the ghee to the pan. Add the fish, skin side down, to the pan, dividing it into batches, if necessary, to avoid crowding the pan. Cook for 1 minute.

If cooking in batches, remove the fish from the pan. Add more ghee, if necessary, and brown the second batch of the fish. Continue until all the salmon has been cooked.

Add all the fish back to the pan and lower the heat to medium. Pour the sauce into the pan and stir to coat the fish. Cook for 1 minute. Transfer the pan to the oven and cook for 4 to 5 minutes, or until cooked through.

Enjoy right away over rice with the Simple Dill Carrot Salad (page 95) or the Perfect Roasted Veggies (page 83), or store in the fridge for 3 to 4 days. Instead of reheating leftovers, I like to eat the salmon cold in a sushi bowl, on a salad or in a seaweed roll!

Healthier Carbohydrates

Carbs are not evil. In fact, they are part of a balanced plate and are an important source of energy. However, it is essential to incorporate quality sources of whole food carbohydrates into your diet and minimize consumption of ultraprocessed carbohydrates, such as refined grains. This chapter has recipes for whole food carbohydrates that are properly prepared to improve digestion and enhance the nutritional value. Different people will feel their best consuming different amounts of carbs, depending on such factors as health status and exercise volume, so experiment and find what works best for you! I always have a loaf of the Gluten-Free Sourdough Sandwich Bread (page 65) in my fridge—the fermentation process gives it a delicious sour flavor and also makes the grains easier to digest. The Prebiotic Potato Salad (page 69) and the Gut-Friendly Herb Rice (page 74) are perfect for meal prep because they actually gain health benefits after sitting in the fridge and they pair perfectly with lots of proteins!

Gluten-Free Sourdough Sandwich Bread

You don't need yeast, starter or hours of kneading to make this magical gluten-free sourdough bread. This recipe uses buckwheat and teff, which are grains that ferment easily, so just leave them in a warm spot for a couple of nights and wild yeast will do its thing. This is a great alternative to more processed gluten-free bread options that have a long list of ingredients that may impact your digestive health. You need just three simple ingredients and water for a delicious loaf of bread! Fermentation not only creates the delicious sourdough flavor but also increases the nutrition of the bread and improves digestibility. The fermentation does take a few nights, so I like to take advantage of my time and double or triple the recipe to prep a few loaves of this flavorful gluten-free sourdough to always have a slice of nutritious bread in my freezer.

Yield: 12 slices

2 cups (340 g) raw buckwheat groats

¾ cup (175 ml) warm filtered water, plus more for soaking

1 cup (180 g) whole-grain teff

¾ tsp sea salt

In a large glass bowl, cover the buckwheat groats with filtered water. Cover with a clean dish towel and let sit in a warm place overnight.

Using a fine-mesh sieve, drain the water but do not rinse the buckwheat.

Transfer the drained buckwheat to a blender and add the teff, ¾ cup (175 ml) of warm filtered water and the sea salt, and blend until fully combined. The mixture should be thick but pourable. Transfer the mixture to the large glass bowl and cover with a dish towel. Let it sit in a warm place for 24 hours.

After 24 hours, the dough should be slightly risen and bubbly. Preheat the oven to 350°F (180°C).

Line an 8 x 4–inch (20 x 10–inch) loaf pan with parchment paper and transfer the dough to the pan. Bake for 90 minutes, or until a knife inserted into the middle comes out clean. Remove from the oven and let cool for 30 to 40 minutes before slicing. It is best enjoyed toasted!

Store in the fridge and serve within 5 to 6 days, or slice the loaf and store in the freezer for 4 to 5 months. To reheat, toast directly from the freezer.

Cheesy Scalloped Potatoes

You'll never want to eat potatoes a different way after you try these warm, cheesy potatoes. They also have some hidden cauliflower in there for any veggie-phobic eaters in your household. They're rich and creamy and the perfect carbohydrate to have in your fridge so that you can warm them up whenever you need to add a quality carb to a plate. Serve them alongside the Easy Roasted Chicken (page 34) and Perfect Roasted Veggies (page 83) for a delicious and satisfying meal.

Yield: 8 servings

4 medium-sized Yukon Gold potatoes

1 leek, sliced thinly

1½ tsp (7 g) unsalted butter, for pan

1 small head cauliflower, chopped finely

Sea salt and freshly ground black pepper

1 cup (120 g) grated Gruyère cheese, divided

1½ cups (355 ml) heavy cream

Pinch of nutmeg, for serving

Preheat your oven to 375°F (190°C).

Thinly slice the potatoes using a sharp knife or mandoline. Slice the leek and soak in water to clean.

Butter a 9-inch (23-cm) cast-iron skillet or 8 x 8–inch (20 x 20–cm) baking dish and layer in the potatoes, leeks and cauliflower, seasoning each layer with salt and pepper.

Once all of the ingredients are layered, sprinkle with half of the cheese and pour in the heavy cream. Cover the dish with a lid or aluminum foil and bake until the potatoes are fork-tender, 45 to 60 minutes.

Remove the cover, add the remaining cheese and broil the dish for 2 to 3 minutes to get a crispy top. Remove from the oven and let sit for at least 30 minutes before serving with a pinch of nutmeg on top.

Store in an airtight container in the fridge for 4 to 5 days. To freeze, divide into portion sizes of your choice and freeze in freezer-safe containers. To reheat, thaw in the fridge overnight and bake in a 350°F (180°C) oven for about 10 minutes, or until warmed through.

Prebiotic Potato Salad

Potato salad can be magical for the gut? Who knew! The gut support comes from the prebiotics that develop in the potatoes when they are cooked and cooled. I also toss in some beans for extra fiber. This is the perfect side dish, or just add a protein source and you have an easy, gut-healthy meal! The best part is you can customize this with your favorite flavors and additions. Add whatever veggies you have on hand, or swap in your favorite herbs. The flavor profiles are endless, so you can meal prep this often without getting tired of it.

Yield: 8 to 10 servings

5 Yukon Gold potatoes, cubed

2 tbsp (36 g) + ½ tsp sea salt, divided

¼ cup (60 ml) extra virgin olive oil

2 tbsp (30 ml) apple cider vinegar

2 tsp (10 g) Dijon mustard

1 shallot, minced

1 cup (180 g) fully cooked or canned and drained cannellini beans

½ cup (90 g) olives, pitted and chopped roughly

½ cup (8 g) fresh cilantro, chopped

Optional additions of choice (fermented peppers, capers, anchovies, fresh herbs)

Place the potatoes in a large pot and cover with cold water. Add the 2 tablespoons (36 g) of sea salt and bring a boil. Lower the heat to a rolling simmer and cook until the potatoes are fork-tender, 10 to 12 minutes.

Remove the potatoes from the heat and drain. Set aside to let cool.

In a large bowl, whisk together the olive oil, apple cider vinegar, mustard, shallot and remaining ½ teaspoon of sea salt.

Toss the cooled potatoes into the bowl that contains the dressing. Add the beans, olives, cilantro and any other additions you like, and toss to combine.

Store in an airtight container in the fridge for 4 to 5 days.

Middle Eastern Lentil Salad

Legumes are a controversial food when it comes to a nutrient-dense diet. While I don't use them as my main source of protein in a meal (the plant protein is not as bioavailable as animal protein), legumes can be useful as a healthy source of carbohydrates. When eating legumes, employing such traditional techniques as soaking and sprouting to properly prepare them can improve digestibility and minimize symptoms like bloating and gas and reduce antinutrients present in lentils, such as phytic acid or other compounds that may interfere with nutrient absorption. This salad is my take on a tabbouleh, but gluten-free and with some added nutrients because it uses lentils in place of the bulgur wheat.

Yield: 6 to 8 servings

1 cup (192 g) dried green or brown lentils

2 cups (475 ml) Simplified Bone Broth (page 30) or water

3 cloves garlic, divided

1 bay leaf

¼ cup (60 ml) extra virgin olive oil

Zest of 1 lemon

2 tbsp (30 ml) fresh lemon juice

1 tsp Dijon mustard

½ tsp sea salt

2 medium-sized cucumbers, diced

2 tomatoes, diced

1 small red onion, diced

1 cup (60 g) fresh parsley, chopped finely

½ cup (75 g) crumbled feta cheese

Rinse the lentils and pick through them to remove any stones or debris. Transfer the lentils to a large bowl and cover with water. Let sit on the counter to soak for 12 hours.

Drain and rinse the lentils. Transfer them to a medium-sized saucepan and cover with the bone broth or water. Add two of the garlic cloves and the bay leaf to the pot. Bring to a boil, then lower the heat to a simmer, cover with a lid and cook for 8 to 10 minutes, stirring occasionally. The lentils are done when they are just tender but not yet getting mushy. Remove from the heat, discard the bay leaf and garlic cloves, drain any remaining liquid and transfer the lentils to a large bowl to let cool for 10 to 15 minutes.

While the lentils cool, make the dressing by combining the olive oil, lemon zest and juice, mustard and sea salt.

Add the cucumbers, tomatoes, red onion, parsley and feta to the bowl of lentils. Pour the dressing over and toss to combine.

Store in an airtight container in the fridge for up to 5 days.

Winter Squash Mash

This creamy, sweet mash is the best way to use up abundant winter squash. Squash is a great, whole food carbohydrate to create a balanced meal. It has a complex flavor that works well with savory flavors but is naturally sweet like a dessert. This simple healthy carb takes just a few minutes of hands-on work and makes a big batch that is perfect for the fridge or the freezer. Make a few batches during the peak of squash season and store it in your fridge to preserve that amazing, comforting winter flavor!

Yield: 10 to 12 servings

1 medium-sized kabocha squash

1 medium-sized butternut squash

1 medium-sized acorn squash

1 tbsp (14 g) ghee, melted

Sea salt

¼ cup (60 g) heavy cream

⅓ cup (76 g/½ stick + 4 tsp) salted butter, melted

½ tsp ground cinnamon

Freshly ground black pepper

Preheat the oven to 350°F (180°C).

Cut each squash in half and scoop out and discard the seeds and pulp from the center. Roughly cut the squash into 2-inch (5-cm)-thick wedges. Coat the squash with ghee and a sprinkle of sea salt, then transfer to a baking sheet and bake until very tender, about 1 hour.

Remove the squash from the oven and let cool until you're able to handle them. Use a spoon to scoop the flesh from the skin. Place the flesh in a large bowl and discard the skin.

Using a hand masher or electric mixer on low speed, mix the squash until smooth. Pour in the cream, melted butter and cinnamon, and mix until incorporated. Season with sea salt and pepper to taste.

Store in the fridge for 4 to 5 days, or freeze in desired portion sizes for 3 to 4 months. To reheat, let thaw in the fridge overnight and heat in a saucepan over medium heat until warmed through.

Gut-Friendly Herb Rice

This vibrant, herby rice is the perfect accompaniment to any protein, which makes it a meal prep staple. The best part about meal prepping rice, or other starchy carbohydrates, is that when rice is cooked and cooled, it develops resistant starch, which is resistant to human digestion, so it feeds our good gut bugs and also makes the starch more blood sugar–friendly. When cooking brown rice, soaking is utilized as a traditional technique to neutralize the antinutrients present in the hull of the rice. Soaking can also be beneficial for white rice, as it reduces arsenic content, which is common in rice crops. Soaking rice takes some forethought and planning, which is why I like to make larger batches and keep it in the fridge or even stock my freezer for a major time-saving hack.

Yield: 8 to 10 servings

2 cups (390 g) uncooked organic white rice

3 cups (710 ml) filtered water

1 tbsp (15 ml) apple cider vinegar

2 cups (475 ml) Simplified Bone Broth (page 30) or water

1 tbsp (14 g) salted butter

Juice of 1 lime

1 cup (60 g) fresh parsley (or equivalent volume of cilantro, basil, dill or other favorite herb)

In a large bowl, cover the rice with the filtered water and mix in the apple cider vinegar. Soak for 3 to 6 hours.

After the soaking time, drain the soaking liquid and rinse the rice two or three times, or until the water runs clear.

If using an Instant Pot: In the inner pot, combine the rice with the bone broth or water, and select the RICE function. Once the cooking is done, manually release the pressure, remove the top and fluff the rice with a fork.

If cooking on the stovetop: In a large saucepan, combine the rice with the bone broth or water. Bring to a boil over medium heat, then lower the heat, cover with a lid and let simmer until the liquid is absorbed into the rice, 8 to 10 minutes. Remove from the heat and fluff with a fork.

Once the rice is fully cooked and has cooled slightly, mix in the butter, lime juice and herbs until well combined.

Store in the fridge for 5 to 6 days, or divide the cooled rice into desired portions and freeze for 2 to 3 months. To reheat, add the rice to any dish and heat it up in the oven, steam it in a pressure cooker or microwave until warmed through.

Fresh Corn Tortillas

Making your own tortillas at home could not be more simple or delicious. The best part about corn tortillas is that masa harina has gone through the nixtamaliza-tion process—a traditional process to properly prepare corn by soaking it in lime water to make it easier to digest. It can be hard to find tortillas in the store with good ingredients, so take 15 minutes of time and mix up your own dough. The process of rolling out dough balls and pressing the tortillas is a fun way to get your whole family involved in the cooking process!

Yield: 24 tortillas

2 cups (224 g) organic masa harina

½ tsp sea salt

1¾ cups (414 ml) hot water, plus more as needed

2 tbsp (28 g) lard, melted (optional)

In a large bowl, combine the masa harina and sea salt. Pour in the hot water and lard (if using), and mix until combined. You want a firm and springy dough. If it is too dry, add more water. If it's too wet, add more masa.

Cover the bowl of dough with a clean kitchen towel and let it rest at room temperature for an hour.

Use your hands to shape the dough into small balls (about the size of golf balls). You should get about 24 balls. Place a dough ball between two pieces of parchment paper, and lightly press in a tortilla press until it forms a tortilla. If you don't have a tortilla press, use a heavy skillet or book to press the ball between two sheets of parchment paper until about 6 inches (15 cm) in diameter.

Heat a dry skillet or griddle over high heat. Peel a tortilla away from the parchment paper and add to the hot skillet or griddle. Cook until lightly browned, 50 to 60 seconds. Flip and cook for another minute on the other side. Repeat the shaping and cooking process with the remaining dough balls.

As you cook the tortillas, keep them in a tortilla warmer or wrapped in a clean kitchen towel so that they do not dry out.

Store the cooked tortillas in an airtight container in the fridge for 3 to 4 days. To freeze, store the pressed uncooked tortillas between parchment paper, seal them in an airtight container and store in the freezer for 2 to 3 months. Whenever you want a fresh tortilla, defrost the tortillas at room temperature and follow the cooking instructions above.

Creamy Squash Soup

This soup is like a warm hug in a bowl—rich and creamy from the squash, without any dairy. The bone broth base adds some quality protein and micronutrients. Serve this alongside your protein at dinner or lunch as a healthy, whole food carbohydrate or add some cooked protein into the soup for a quick, balanced meal.

Yield: 6 to 8 servings

1 medium-sized butternut squash, cut in half lengthwise

1 medium-sized acorn squash, cut in half lengthwise

1 tbsp (14 ml) extra virgin olive oil

2 tsp (5 g) ground cinnamon

1½ tsp (9 g) sea salt, divided

1 yellow onion, peeled and quartered

1 head garlic, cut in half

1 qt (946 ml) Simplified Bone Broth (page 30)

1 tbsp (2 g) fresh rosemary leaves

1½ tsp (1 g) fresh thyme leaves

Preheat your oven to 350°F (180°C).

Remove the seeds from the center of each squash and discard. Season the squash with the olive oil, cinnamon and 1 teaspoon of the sea salt, then place, flesh side down, on a baking sheet. Add the onion and garlic, cut side down, to the baking sheet.

Roast for 50 to 60 minutes, or until the squash is fork-tender. Remove from the oven and let sit until cool enough to handle. Then, use a spoon to separate the squash flesh from the skin. Discard the skin.

In a large pot, combine the bone broth, rosemary and thyme over medium heat and heat until warm. Add the squash flesh, onion, garlic and remaining ½ teaspoon of sea salt to the pot, then use an immersion blender or transfer to a blender and blend until creamy. Taste and adjust the seasonings as needed.

Store in the fridge for 4 to 5 days. To freeze, divide into desired portion sizes and freeze in an airtight container for 3 to 5 months. To reheat, let thaw in the fridge and cook in a saucepan over medium heat until warmed through.

Versatile Veggies

Eating a wide variety of produce is one of the best things you can do for your health. These foods provide a range of nutrients, including beneficial antioxidants and phytonutrients, and ensure you have a healthy, diverse gut microbiome. I put together these easy, delicious and fridge- and freezer-friendly veggies so that you can also have a veggie on hand to add to your plate. For those who are working on improving their gut health, it can be helpful to replace raw veggies that can be hard to digest with vegetables that have been prepared to improve digestibility, such as fermented or cooked veggies. We also want dishes that will store well in the fridge, so instead of salads that will get soggy, we will focus on fermented veggies, roasted veggies that can easily be crisped up, braised vegetables and hearty ingredients, such as beets and carrots. I love to ferment a few seasonal veggies, using my Lacto-Fermented Veggies recipe (page 87) for a delicious, gut-healthy addition to any meal that lasts for months in the fridge. The Bone Broth Braised Greens (page 88) use an easy method that can make the nutrients in any leafy green easier to absorb, and my Simple Dill Carrot Salad (page 95) is a fridge staple that I add to my meals for its hormone health benefits.

Perfect Roasted Veggies

*This simplified formula will make roasting veggies straightforward and success-
ful every time. You don't need a whole new recipe for every vegetable—feel free
to swap in different veggies that you have on hand or that are in season. For
example, in the spring I love to combine asparagus, zucchini and radishes. For
a summer spread, try tomatoes, bell peppers, summer squash and onions. In
the winter, sweet potatoes, winter squash, Brussels sprouts and parsnips are
great roasting options. Just ensure that the veggies you choose cook at relatively
similar timelines and are cut uniformly so that everything is cooked evenly. Having
veggies prepped in your fridge dramatically increases your chance of consuming
them—so make a big batch and have this in the fridge to add to any meal or just
serve them with a delicious dip, such as my Creamy Caesar Dip (page 151).*

Yield: 8 servings

4 carrots

2 sweet potatoes

1 cauliflower

1 yellow onion

2 tbsp (28 g) salted butter,
or ghee or coconut oil,
melted

1½ tsp (2 g) dried oregano

1 tsp sea salt

Preheat the oven to 375°F (190°C).

Chop up the carrots, sweet potatoes, cauliflower and onion.
Make sure the chopped pieces are similar sizes so they cook
evenly. Spread out the veggies on a baking sheet.

Mix the melted butter with the oregano and sea salt (or other
seasonings of choice).

Coat the veggies with the seasoned butter, tossing to make
sure they are evenly coated. Bake for 20 minutes, or until the
veggies are fork-tender. To finish, broil for 2 to 3 minutes, or
until browned and crispy.

Store in an airtight container in the fridge for 5 to 6 days.
To freeze, divide into desired portion sizes and freeze in a
freezer-safe container. To reheat, thaw in the fridge overnight and heat in a hot skillet or bake in a 350°F (180°C) oven
until warmed through, then finish under the broiler for 1 to
2 minutes to crisp up.

Easy 30-Minute Sauerkraut

Sauerkraut—fermented cabbage—is an amazing dish to master at home. By combining cabbage with sea salt and letting it sit on the counter for a couple of weeks, you can transform this humble veggie into a tangy, probiotic-rich snack that adds flavor and gut-health benefits to any meal. Learning to make your own sauerkraut at home will save you a ton of money because a quality sauerkraut is pricey. Keep it simple with just cabbage and salt, or add typical kraut spices or other veggies such as shaved carrots. Just a spoonful each day can provide great gut-health support and it's easy to add to any meal! I recommend weighing the measurements for this in metrics, rather than using US measurements by volume, to ensure the amounts are perfect.

Yield: 1 (½-gal [1.9-L]) jar

---

2 lb + 14 oz (1.3 kg) green cabbage (roughly 1 large head), chopped/shredded finely

1 tbsp + 2½ tsp (33 g) sea salt

1 tbsp (about a 15-ml volume) kraut spices (dill, caraway, juniper berry, mustard seeds or coriander) (optional)

In a large bowl, combine the shredded cabbage with the sea salt. Massage the cabbage and sea salt for 5 to 7 minutes, or until the cabbage starts to break down and release liquid. Cover the bowl with a clean towel and let it sit for 15 minutes to allow more liquid to release.

After 15 minutes, add your spices or herbs of choice to the cabbage and use your hands to mix it well.

Pack the cabbage tightly into a clean half-gallon (1.9-L) jar, using your fist or a wooden tamper, leaving 1 to 2 inches (2.5 to 5 cm) of headspace from the top of the vessel. All the cabbage should be submerged in liquid. If there is not enough liquid, add just enough water to submerge everything.

Use a ceramic or glass fermenting weight (or other creative, nonmetal weight) to keep the cabbage submerged in liquid. Cover the jar loosely with a lid. Or, if you are using an airlock lid, add water into the airlock chamber and secure the lid onto the jar. Let it ferment in a dark spot (out of direct sunlight) at room temperature for a minimum of 5 days, then taste every 2 days to reach the desired flavor. Kraut can ferment for up to 30 days for a sourer flavor. Transfer into the refrigerator to store for 6 to 12 months.

Lacto-Fermented Veggies

Turn almost any veggie into a delicious, gut-friendly natural probiotic with this easy formula. Lacto-fermentation is the process of bacteria breaking down sugars in foods and forming lactic acid. Just choose your veggies—some of my favorites are carrots, radishes, cucumbers, turnips and/or green beans—chop them up, then submerge them in a 2.5 to 3 percent salt water brine using the formula in this recipe. Sea salt keeps unwanted bacteria from growing in your ferment, allowing the good bacteria to flourish. It plays another important role in keeping the veggies crisp, because no one likes a soggy vegetable. Not only does fermentation introduce good bacteria that can support a healthy microbiome, it is also a great way to improve digestibility, so if raw veggies make you bloated or mess with your digestion, try fermenting them!

Yield: 10 servings

Organic veggies of choice (carrots, green beans, radishes, turnips, beets, cucumbers, peppers, cauliflower, cabbage, garlic)

Filtered water

Fresh herbs or spices

Sea salt

Note: If you notice mold on your fermentation or it smells off, discard the entire mixture and start again.

Wash and chop your veggies into your desired sizes and shapes.

Place your sanitized fermenting jar on a kitchen scale, and zero out the scale. Add your chopped veggies to the jar, cover with filtered water and add any herbs or spices you desire. Take this measurement of the veggies and water in grams and multiply by 0.025 to 0.03 to determine the amount of salt needed in grams. Crisp veggies, such as carrots and turnips, will need less salt, whereas soft or sweeter veggies, such as cucumbers and beets, will need closer to 3 percent brine to prevent mold and keep the veggie crisp. Set the jar aside.

Place a bowl on the kitchen scale and zero out the scale. In the bowl, measure the amount of salt needed, then pour the water from the jar of veggies into the bowl. Stir until the salt is fully dissolved. This is your fermenting brine.

Pour the fermenting brine back into the jar of veggies. Use a fermenting weight or another heavy, nonmetal object to make sure all the veggies are submerged in the water. Cover with a fermenting airlock lid or a jar lid that is not fully tightened so that air can escape. Store in a place between 60 and 75°F (16 and 25°C) and taste after 5 to 30 days of fermenting. Once it has reached your desired flavor, store it in the fridge for up to a year.

Most veggies can be fermented. Play around with different veggie and spice combos. All you need is the equation: (the weight of the veggie + the weight of the water) x 0.025 to 0.03 = salt needed (in grams).

Bone Broth Braised Greens

Make your veggies even more flavorful, nutritious and gut friendly when you cook them in nutrient-rich bone broth. Cooking veggies breaks down the tough cellular structure, making them easier to digest. Cooking may also reduce anti-nutrients found in some veggies, such as oxalates, which may inhibit absorption of certain nutrients. Therefore, not only does cooking veggies mean you may reduce your symptoms of bloating or indigestion, but the nutrients are easier to digest and absorb. Adding ghee as a healthy fat will also improve nutrient content since it improves absorption of fat-soluble vitamins. Cooking these greens in bone broth adds a rich, savory flavor that is perfectly complemented with a squeeze of fresh lemon juice!

Yield: 6 servings

1½ tsp (21 g) ghee

½ yellow onion, diced

5 cloves garlic, minced

2 bunches rainbow chard or collard greens, chopped

¼ cup (60 ml) Simplified Bone Broth (page 30)

Sea salt

Juice of ½ lemon

In a large skillet, melt the ghee over medium heat. Add the onion and garlic, and sauté over medium heat until translucent and fragrant, 3 to 4 minutes.

Add the greens and the bone broth to the pan. Stir to incorporate. Add a pinch of salt. Cover the pan and cook until the greens are wilted and the bone broth has cooked down, 10 to 12 minutes.

Finish with a squeeze of lemon juice and more salt to taste. Store in an airtight container in the fridge for 4 to 5 days.

Rustic French Ratatouille

This classic French dish is an easy way to prep a bunch of fresh produce that is abundant during summer months. It's a delicious way to have veggies prepped in your fridge because it gets tastier as it sits! After just 30 minutes of effort, you're left with a versatile dish that you can heat on the stove or even eat cold! Serve it with the Easy Roasted Chicken (page 34) for a simple and healthy meal that will transport you to a vacation in France.

Yield: 8 to 10 servings

---

1 large eggplant, cut into 1" (2.5-cm) cubes

Sea salt

3½ tbsp (52 ml) extra virgin olive oil, divided

1 red onion, medium diced

4 cloves garlic, minced

1½ lb (680 g) Roma tomatoes, chopped roughly

1 tsp dried oregano

½ tsp red pepper flakes

1 large zucchini, chopped roughly

1 yellow summer squash, chopped roughly

Freshly ground black pepper

Fresh basil, for serving

Place the eggplant in a colander over a bowl or sink and sprinkle with 1 teaspoon of sea salt. This will allow it to drain excess liquid while you prep the other ingredients.

Meanwhile, in a Dutch oven or large pot, heat 1½ teaspoons (7 ml) of the olive oil over medium heat. Add the red onion and garlic, and sauté until fragrant, 3 to 4 minutes.

Add the tomatoes to the pot and stir. Add ½ teaspoon of sea salt plus the oregano and red pepper flakes. Lower the heat to medium-low, cover the pot and let cook, stirring occasionally, for 10 to 15 minutes, or until the tomatoes are broken down into a sauce. Transfer the sauce to a bowl and set aside.

In the same pot, heat 1 tablespoon (15 ml) of the olive oil over medium heat. Dry off the eggplant, add it to the pot and cook for 3 to 4 minutes, or until it's beginning to soften and lightly brown. Transfer the eggplant to a bowl and set aside.

Add the remaining tablespoon (15 ml) of olive oil to the pot, add the zucchini and summer squash and cook for 3 to 4 minutes, or until they begin to soften and brown. Add the eggplant back to the pot. Add the tomato sauce to the pot and stir to combine. Lower the heat to low, cover with a lid and let simmer for 20 to 30 minutes, or until the vegetables are tender.

Season to taste with salt and black pepper and top with fresh basil. If you are prepping in advance, reserve the fresh basil and add when you are serving.

Keep in the fridge for 4 to 5 days. To freeze, cool completely and store in the freezer in an airtight container in desired portion sizes for 2 to 3 months. To serve, thaw in the refrigerator and reheat on the stovetop.

Heart-Healthy Beet Salad

Salads can be hard to meal prep because they will get soggy and wilted in the fridge. Choosing hearty veggies, such as beets, is a great way to meal prep veggies because they hold up in the fridge well. Beets have some amazing health benefits, too—they are known to support heart health and have anti-inflammatory effects. Here, they are paired with bright grapefruit, fennel and basil for a tangy, fresh flavor. Serve this salad right away and store the rest in the fridge to add a delicious veggie to your meals during the week.

Yield: 8 servings

4 large beets, greens removed

3 grapefruits, peeled and sectioned

1 small fennel bulb, shaved thinly

½ cup (20 g) fresh basil leaves, chopped roughly

3 tbsp (45 ml) extra virgin olive oil

1 tbsp (15 ml) apple cider vinegar

1 tsp Dijon mustard

¼ tsp sea salt

Thoroughly wash the beets. If cooking on the stovetop, place them in a steamer basket and steam the beats until fork-tender, 45 to 60 minutes. If using a pressure cooker, place them on a trivet in the pressure cooker with 1 cup (240 ml) of water and pressure cook for 25 minutes. Let it naturally release for 10 minutes, then manually release.

Once fork-tender, transfer the beets to an ice bath and use your hands to peel off the skins. Cut the peeled beets into 2-inch (5-cm) pieces and place in a large bowl with the grapefruit, fennel and basil leaves.

In a small bowl, make the dressing by combining the olive oil, apple cider vinegar, mustard and sea salt and whisk well. Add the dressing to the bowl of beets and toss to combine.

Store in an airtight container in the fridge for 4 to 5 days.

Simple Dill Carrot Salad

This is an easy way to add some fresh veggies and fiber to any meal. This salad is another option for meal prep because it stores well in the fridge throughout the week. Raw carrots have a unique fiber that binds excess estrogen and eliminates toxins, which supports healthy hormone balance. Aside from that, it's an easy way to quickly add soluble and insoluble fiber to a meal, supporting regular digestion, which is also key to healthy hormones. Plus, this is a crunchy salad that the whole family will love!

Yield: 5 servings

2 tbsp (30 ml) extra virgin olive oil

1 tbsp (15 ml) coconut oil, melted

1 tbsp (15 ml) apple cider vinegar

1 tsp Dijon mustard

½ tsp sea salt

5 medium-sized carrots

3 tbsp (12 g) fresh dill, chopped

In a large bowl, make the dressing by mixing the olive oil, coconut oil, apple cider vinegar, mustard and sea salt until incorporated.

Use a vegetable peeler to shave the carrots directly into the bowl that contains the dressing. Add the dill and toss to combine with the dressing until fully coated.

Serve immediately or store in the fridge for up to 5 days.

Protein-Rich Breakfasts

Eating a savory, protein-rich breakfast is one of the best ways to support balanced blood sugar levels, which has so many downstream effects—better energy, steady mood, improved hormone balance and reduced cravings later in the day. Plus, if you don't eat breakfast, you will likely struggle to meet your daily protein goals. If you're scrambling (pun intended) to get out of the house in the morning, prepping a quality breakfast will help you stay on track with your nutrient-dense diet so you don't have to lean on protein bars or sugary muffins. This section includes plenty of breakfast options that you can prepare in advance and store in the fridge or freezer, such as my go-to Single-Serving Frittatas (page 99) and the crowd favorite High-Protein Pancakes (page 115). If you like to prepare breakfast fresh each morning, I have included a few nutrient-rich options that take only 5 to 10 minutes, such as my 5-Minute Bone Broth Breakfast Soup (page 104) and Balanced Smoothie Formula (page 103)!

Single-Serving Frittata

You'll never miss a breakfast or reach for an unsatisfying protein bar when you master these Single-Serving Frittatas. They are the perfect on-the-go or quick breakfast, rich in protein to keep your blood sugar stable and reduce cravings throughout your day. The cottage cheese keeps these creamy and fluffy while adding some extra protein. Feel free to experiment with seasonal veggies and different meats and cheeses for varying combinations; just make sure any additions are fully cooked before baking into muffins so that everything is cooked through at the end.

Yield: 12 muffins

---

1 tbsp (14 g) beef tallow or ghee, plus more for muffin tin

½ yellow onion, diced

3 cloves garlic, minced

8 oz (225 g) ground chorizo or other ground meat

2 cups (70 g) tightly packed raw spinach

12 large eggs

½ cup (115 g) cottage cheese (optional)

½ tsp sea salt

2 tsp (4 g) freshly ground black pepper (optional)

Preheat the oven to 350°F (180°C). Grease a 12-well muffin tin with tallow.

In a large skillet, heat the tallow over medium heat. Add the onion and garlic, and sauté until fragrant, 3 to 4 minutes.

Increase the heat to medium-high and add the ground chorizo. Use a wooden spoon to break up the meat, then sauté until cooked through, 7 to 8 minutes. Stir in the spinach and cook until the spinach is fully cooked, 3 to 4 minutes. Remove from the heat and set aside.

In a large bowl, whisk the eggs. Add the cottage cheese (if using), sea salt and pepper (if using), and stir to combine.

Once the chorizo and spinach mixture has cooled slightly, add it to the egg mixture and stir to combine. Divide the mixture equally among the 12 wells of the prepared muffin tin and bake for 20 to 25 minutes, or until cooked through.

Serve immediately or let cool before storing. Store in an airtight container in the fridge for 3 to 4 days. To freeze, store in an airtight container for up to 4 months. To reheat, let thaw in the fridge overnight, then reheat in a 325°F (170°C) oven for 7 to 8 minutes, or until warmed through.

Mini Meat Muffins

If you want a savory, protein-rich breakfast that doesn't include eggs or dairy, this is the dish for you! Packed with quality protein from the meat, these flavorful muffins are perfect for a busy morning or if you need to pack breakfast to go. They reheat quickly but are also delicious cold! A few of these for your morning meal will keep you satisfied for hours and help you reach your protein goals for optimal health.

Yield: 12 muffins

1½ tsp (21 g) ghee or beef tallow

½ yellow onion, diced

4 cloves garlic, minced

2 bell peppers, seeded and diced

8 oz (225 g) cremini mushrooms, sliced

1½ lb (680 g) ground beef

2 tsp (8 g) grass-fed beef gelatin powder

2 tsp (12 g) sea salt

½ cup (60 g) Cheddar cheese (optional)

Preheat the oven to 350°F (180°C). Line a 12-well muffin tin with liners.

Heat a skillet over medium-high heat. Add the ghee and let it melt. Add the onion and garlic, and sauté until translucent and fragrant, about 3 minutes.

Stir in the bell peppers and mushrooms, then cook, stirring occasionally, until cooked through and tender, about 10 minutes. Remove from the heat and let cool slightly.

In a large bowl, combine the cooked veggies, ground beef, gelatin and sea salt. Stir in the cheese here if you are including it.

Divide equally among the prepared muffin wells and bake until cooked through, 30 to 35 minutes.

If not serving immediately, let cool before storing. Store in an airtight container in the fridge for 3 to 4 days. To freeze, store in an airtight container for up to 4 months. To reheat, let thaw in the fridge overnight, then reheat in a 325°F (170°C) oven for 7 to 8 minutes, or until warmed through.

Balanced Smoothie Formula

A smoothie can be a solid, quick breakfast option, if it is made with quality ingredients. Rather than packing these with sugary fruits that can spike blood sugar and lead to an energy roller coaster, mood swings and cravings later in the day, the protein, healthy fats and fiber of a balanced smoothie will keep you full and satiated and minimize the glucose response. When formulating a smoothie, aim for at least 25 grams of quality protein from such sources as Greek yogurt or a high-quality protein powder, healthy fats and lower-sugar fruits, such as berries.

Here are two balanced smoothie options—the Blueberry Cheesecake is fruity and creamy, while the Vitamin C–Avocado has a tart, refreshing flavor! These simple smoothies only take about five minutes to whip up, but if you want to make them more meal prep friendly, batch all the ingredients, except for the liquid, in a bag or container to store in the freezer, then blend with your liquid of choice each morning.

Yield: 1 smoothie

Blueberry Cheesecake

½ cup (120 ml) milk of choice or water

¼ cup (55 g) cottage cheese

¼ cup (45 g) frozen coconut

¼ cup (39 g) frozen blueberries

1 serving unflavored or vanilla collagen powder or protein powder of choice

Vitamin C-Avocado

½ cup (120 ml) kefir, milk of choice, coconut water or water

½ lemon, peeled and seeded

1 (1" [2.5-cm]) piece organic fresh ginger

1 tsp camu camu powder or acerola cherry powder

½ cup (50 g) frozen avocado

1 serving vanilla or unflavored protein powder

¼ frozen banana (optional)

Whether you make the Blueberry Cheesecake or the Vitamin C –Avocado flavor, simply combine all the ingredients for your desired smoothie in a blender and blend until smooth.

5-Minute Bone Broth Breakfast Soup

A warm, nourishing breakfast in five minutes sounds impossible, but this recipe gets quality protein from my Simplified Bone Broth (page 30) and eggs, as well as uses other kitchen staples so you can whip up a comforting breakfast in the time that your coffee brews. While it does take five minutes of cooking time in the morning, it comes together with minimal effort if you have bone broth prepped and ready to go. This is a great breakfast if you don't feel like you can stomach much food in the morning, because it's a light, easy-to-digest meal that still packs great nutrients!

Yield: 1 serving

1½ cups (355 ml) Simplified Bone Broth (page 30)

1 (1" [2.5-cm]) piece fresh ginger, peeled

1 clove garlic, peeled

2 large eggs

1 green onion, sliced

1 tsp tamari

Toasted sesame oil (optional)

Pour the bone broth into a small saucepan. Grate the ginger and garlic directly into the pot. Heat the broth over medium heat.

Meanwhile, crack the eggs into a bowl and whisk lightly. Once the broth starts to boil, add half of the green onion to the pot, reserving the rest for garnish. Stir the broth to create a whirlpool and slowly pour the whisked eggs into the pot, continuing to stir.

Once you have poured in all of the egg mixture, remove the soup from the heat and serve in a bowl. Top with the remaining green onion and season with the tamari and sesame oil (if using).

Savory Masa Bowl

This dish resembles a comforting bowl of corn grits, but it actually uses masa harina, which is a little easier on the gut because the corn is nixtamalized—a traditional process of soaking the corn in lime, which makes it easier to digest. The base comes together in just five minutes and you can use leftovers, such as beef, chicken or seafood, to add quality protein to the dish. Top it with an over-easy or soft-boiled egg for a delicious, runny yolk that packs great nutrients. If you have limited time in the morning, prep a larger batch of the masa harina and have your protein prepped so that all you have to do is assemble the bowl each morning.

Yield: 1 serving

---

1 cup (240 ml) Simplified Bone Broth (page 30), milk or water

⅓ cup (37 g) organic masa harina

1½ tsp (7 g) salted butter

Sea salt

Precooked protein of choice (eggs, meat, seafood)

Chives, green onions or pickled onions, for serving (optional)

In a small saucepan, bring the bone broth to a boil. Stir in the masa harina, then stir vigorously.

Lower the heat to medium-low and let cook for 5 to 6 minutes while stirring continuously, or until thick and cooked through. Remove from the heat and stir in the butter and sea salt.

Add any toppings, such as fried eggs, poached eggs, boiled eggs, meat or seafood.

Sprinkle with some chives, green onions or pickled onions, if you'd like.

Make-Ahead Protein Oatmeal

Oatmeal is a staple breakfast in many households, but if you want it to be a blood sugar–friendly meal, you need to ensure it includes quality protein and healthy fats. This batch recipe is easy to freeze and sneaks some eggs into the mix, which makes the oatmeal creamy and delicious and adds such essential nutrients as quality protein, B vitamins and healthy fats. I also recommend using organic oats and choosing a sprouted oat, which can reduce antinutrients and improve digestibility.

Yield: 8 servings

6 cups (1.4 L) water

1 tsp sea salt

3 cups (240 g) organic rolled oats (spouted is ideal)

4 large eggs

2 tbsp (28 g) salted butter

1 tsp vanilla extract

1 tsp ground cinnamon

1 tsp ground ginger

Berries, Greek yogurt, protein powder, chia seeds, chopped nuts, for serving (optional)

In a medium-sized saucepan, bring the water and salt to a boil. Stir in the oats and lower the heat to medium-low. Cook for about 10 minutes, stirring occasionally. Once the oatmeal is cooked, remove from the heat and set aside to cool.

In a medium-sized bowl, whisk the eggs. Slowly incorporate the warm oatmeal into the bowl of eggs while stirring constantly to avoid curdling your eggs. Once you have incorporated about 1 cup (240 g) of the cooked oatmeal into the eggs, transfer the egg mixture to the pot containing the rest of the oatmeal and cook over medium-low heat for 3 to 4 minutes while stirring continuously. Remove from the heat and stir in the butter, vanilla, cinnamon and ginger.

Serve the oatmeal with any toppings you like, such as berries, Greek yogurt, protein powder, seeds or nuts.

Store in the fridge for up to 4 days. To freeze, divide into desired portion sizes and freeze for 3 to 4 months. To reheat, thaw the oatmeal in the fridge overnight and reheat in a saucepan over medium heat until cooked through.

Breakfast Fried Rice

This simplified take on fried rice is the perfect savory, balanced breakfast meal. The big bonus is that it relies on leftovers you need to use up from your fridge— cooked rice and a serving of leftover protein transform into a unique breakfast dish for when you're tired of hard-boiled eggs and omelets. Whip up a larger batch at the beginning of the week or fry it all together fresh each morning, since it only takes about eight minutes total.

Yield: 1 serving

1 tbsp (14 g) ghee or beef tallow, divided

⅓ cup (57 g) leftover cooked rice

2 to 3 oz (57 to 85 g) fully cooked meat

2 or 3 large eggs

1½ tsp (8 ml) organic tamari or coconut aminos

Heat a large skillet over medium heat and add 1½ teaspoons (7 g) of the ghee. Stir in your rice and let heat for 2 to 3 minutes. Add your meat of choice and stir to combine. Push the mixture to the side of your pan.

Add the remaining 1½ teaspoons (7 g) of ghee to the empty side of the pan and crack in your eggs. Stir until they are almost fully cooked, then combine with the rice and meat mixture.

Remove from the heat and season with the tamari. Serve with Lacto-Fermented Veggies (page 87) or the Simple Dill Carrot Salad (page 95)!

Cottage Cheese Breakfast Parfait

If you prefer a sweet breakfast but still want the health benefits of quality protein in the morning, this is for you. This protein-rich parfait is perfect for prepping a few breakfasts that you can pick up from the fridge and eat on the go or pack for work. For extra protein, add a quality collagen peptide or protein powder. Make a sweeter version with seasonal fruit and nuts, or try the savory Mediterranean option for a fresh, nourishing breakfast. Whip up a batch of the base and make two of each flavor so that you can switch up your breakfasts each morning and keep it interesting!

Yield: 6 servings

Base
15 oz (425 g) cottage cheese

2 cups (460 g) Greek yogurt

3 servings unflavored collagen or protein powder (optional)

Berry
¼ cup (55 g) Simple Fruit Jam (page 154)

¼ cup (34 g) macadamia nuts, chopped

Banana Cream
1 banana, sliced

¼ cup (34 g) macadamia nuts, chopped

Savory Mediterranean
2 Roma tomatoes, diced

1 cucumber, diced

5 fresh basil leaves, chopped

In a blender or food processor, combine the cottage cheese, Greek yogurt and protein powder (if using) until fully combined and smooth.

Layer the cottage cheese mixture with your additions of choice in six 8-ounce (240-ml) glass Mason jars. Secure the lids and store in the fridge for 5 to 6 days.

High-Protein Pancakes

Your pancake breakfast just got a little more blood sugar friendly and nourishing with these protein-packed pancakes. The best part is you can't even taste the cottage cheese—these taste and feel like the fluffy pancakes your family loves. The cottage cheese and eggs add quality protein and nutrients and keeps the pancakes moist and fluffy. Make a few batches and freeze the fully cooked pancakes for an easy, fun breakfast treat without much cooking.

Yield: 8 to 10 pancakes

3 large eggs

¾ cup (169 g) cottage cheese

2 tbsp (30 ml) pure maple syrup

⅓ cup (40 g) cassava flour

1 tsp baking powder

1 tsp vanilla extract

Pinch of sea salt

2 tbsp (28 g) ghee, plus more as needed

Berries, Greek yogurt, butter, maple syrup, for serving (optional)

In a large bowl, stir together the eggs, cottage cheese and maple syrup until smooth. Stir in the cassava flour, baking powder, vanilla and sea salt until fully combined.

Heat a skillet over medium-low heat and add 1½ teaspoons (7 g) of ghee to the pan. Scoop ¼ cup (60 ml) of the pancake batter onto the skillet and cook for 2 to 3 minutes, or until bubbles form on the top. Flip and cook on the other side for another 1 to 2 minutes. Remove from the pan, add more ghee as needed and continue with the rest of the batter.

Serve immediately with toppings of choice, such as fresh berries, yogurt, butter and maple syrup.

To freeze, line a baking sheet with parchment paper and place the cooled pancakes on it in a single layer. Freeze until solid and then transfer to an airtight, freezer-safe container. To reheat, let the pancakes thaw overnight or reheat straight from the freezer in a 325°F (170°C) oven until warmed through.

Clean-the-Fridge Omelet

An omelet feels like a classic breakfast—and for good reason! It's a simple, savory, protein-filled meal that will keep you satisfied for hours. You can add extra veggies, meat and cheese for fun combos and delicious bites. It's also a great way to clear out leftovers. If you find yourself with leftover cooked veggies and meat, toss together this everything-but-the-kitchen-sink omelet for a quick, satisfying breakfast that will keep your blood sugar steady and help you reach your protein goals.

Yield: 1 serving

---

3 large eggs

Sea salt

1 tbsp (14 g) salted butter

⅓ cup (4 oz [115 g]) cooked veggies (I love this with my leftover Bone Broth Braised Greens [page 88] or Perfect Roasted Veggies [page 83])

⅓ cup (4 oz [115 g]) fully cooked leftover protein (I love this with leftover Family-Size Pork Carnitas [page 55])

¼ cup (30 g) shredded Cheddar cheese (this is also great with goat cheese or feta)

In a bowl, combine the eggs and a pinch of salt and whisk well. Heat a small skillet over medium heat and add the butter to the pan.

Once the butter is melted, add the eggs to the pan and stir for 10 seconds, then allow the egg to cook undisturbed, to set, for 1 minute.

Add your veggies, protein and cheese to one side of the egg. Once the egg is mostly cooked through, fold the egg in half. Let cook for 30 more seconds, then remove from the heat and serve.

Serve as is or top it with one of my favorite sauces, such as Budget-Friendly Pesto (page 153), Chimichurri (page 158) or Fermented Hot Sauce (page 161).

Decadent (and Nutrient-Dense!) Desserts

Dessert can be decadent *and* nutrient dense! I don't believe there are any "bad" foods—just bad ingredients and bad ways to make them. So, let's whip up some of your favorite treats with real, whole food ingredients. It's also helpful to incorporate healthy fats, such as coconut, quality dairy and protein—from such ingredients as eggs and collagen—in desserts to minimize glucose spikes that can cause fatigue, cravings and even chronic health conditions. All the desserts you find in this chapter are naturally and minimally sweetened and packed with nutrients while still being incredibly tasty. When you make my nutrient-dense desserts, you can enjoy your favorite foods and still feel your best! My famous Creamy Nutrient-Dense Ice Cream (page 122) is a fan favorite that packs beneficial fat-soluble nutrients, including vitamins A, D and K from the eggs, as well as quality dairy. The Grain-Free Chocolate Chip Cookies (page 134) are made with the best ingredients but still satisfy a craving for a classic chocolate chip cookie. If you're looking for a gluten- and dairy-free option, check out my tart and creamy Single-Serving Key Lime Pie (page 138).

High-Protein Pot de Crème

This decadent chocolate mousse comes together in a few minutes with the help of a blender or food processor. It's the easiest chocolate dessert to make and packs some extra nutrients from the cottage cheese and grass-fed gelatin. It's minimally sweetened, plus adding protein to your desserts is a great way to blunt the blood sugar response from eating sweets. That also means this irresistible single-serving pot de crème can double as a sweet afternoon snack!

Yield: 5 servings

1 cup (225 g) cottage cheese

½ cup (120 ml) milk

½ cup (120 ml) heavy cream

3 to 4 tbsp (18 to 24 g) unsweetened raw cacao powder

2 to 4 tbsp (30 to 60 ml) pure maple syrup or raw honey, depending on sweetness preference

1 tbsp (10 g) grass-fed beef gelatin powder

½ cup (120 ml) whipping cream, for serving

In a blender or food processor, combine the cottage cheese, milk, heavy cream, cacao powder, maple syrup and beef gelatin, and blend until smooth. Taste and add more cacao powder or sweetener as needed.

Divide equally among five small glass jars or ramekins. In a medium-sized bowl, using an electric hand mixer, or in a stand mixer, whip the whipping cream until it thickens and forms medium-stiff peaks.

Enjoy the pot de crème right away or chill before serving with a dollop of the homemade whipped cream.

Store in the fridge in an airtight container for up to 5 days.

Creamy Nutrient-Dense Ice Cream

Who says ice cream can't be a superfood? When you make it at home with the right ingredients, ice cream can actually be one of the best desserts when it comes to nutrient density. Egg yolks are where you find most of the great nutrients that eggs have to offer, including vitamins A, D, E, K and B vitamins, plus they are a good source of healthy fat. My version is naturally sweetened with a minimal amount of raw honey or maple syrup, which makes it more blood sugar–friendly than your typical ice cream without sacrificing any of the creamy, delicious flavor.

Yield: 8 servings

4 large egg yolks

½ tsp vanilla bean paste

¼ cup (60 ml) raw honey or pure maple syrup

Pinch of sea salt

2 cups (475 ml) heavy cream

1 cup (240 ml) whole milk

Chocolate chips, fresh fruit, mint extract or cookies (optional)

In a large bowl, combine the egg yolks, vanilla bean paste, honey and salt. Stir until well mixed. Add the heavy cream and milk to the bowl and whisk to incorporate.

If you have an ice-cream maker, you can transfer the mixture to the device and follow the manufacturer's instructions.

For a no-churn version, lightly whip the mixture with an electric hand mixer or stand mixer, then place the mixture in a glass food storage container and cover with a lid, leaving at least 2 inches (5 cm) of headspace. Place the container in the freezer and remove the ice cream every hour for the first few hours to stir the contents for a creamier texture. Freeze for 8 hours or overnight.

For the best texture, remove the ice cream from the freezer about 10 minutes before you want to eat it. This is best consumed within 3 to 4 weeks, but I don't think you'll have a problem doing that!

Gut-Healing Maple Marshmallows

These marshmallows are packed with ingredients that have some gut-healing properties and don't contain any of the harmful ingredients usually found in marshmallows. Beef gelatin is made from beef bones and connective tissue—this is a great source of quality protein and a wide range of amino acids that have been found to support a healthy gut lining. Unlike store-bought marshmallows that are loaded with refined sugar, these are minimally and naturally sweetened. Plus, these marshmallows actually incorporate marshmallow root—an herb that has been found to help heal the gut lining and help with digestive issues.

Yield: 8 to 10 marshmallows

Coconut oil, for coating

2 cups (475 ml) water

1 tbsp (15 g) marshmallow root (see note)

¼ cup (40 g) grass-fed beef gelatin powder

¾ cup (175 ml) pure maple syrup

Pinch of sea salt

1 tsp vanilla extract

Notes: Marshmallow root may be available in a bulk section of your local grocery store or natural food store. If not, order from a quality online source, such as Mountain Rose Herbs®.

Coat an 8 x 8–inch (20 x 20–cm) glass dish with parchment paper and coat the parchment paper with coconut oil. Set aside.

Start by making a marshmallow root decoction: In a small saucepan, combine the water with the marshmallow root. Bring it to a boil, then lower the heat to a simmer and cook, uncovered, for 20 minutes, or until the water has reduced by half. Remove from the heat and strain through a fine-mesh sieve. Use the back of a spoon to press down on the herb and extract all of the liquid. Set the mixture aside and let it cool completely.

Into the bowl of a stand mixer fitted with the whisk attachment, pour ½ cup (120 ml) of the cooled marshmallow decoction, then sprinkle the gelatin over it and let it bloom.

While it blooms, in a large saucepan, combine the remaining ½ cup (120 ml) of the marshmallow root decoction plus the maple syrup and sea salt. Bring to a boil, then reduce the heat and let it simmer for about 10 minutes.

Turn the stand mixer on low speed to break up the bloomed gelatin. Remove the syrup from the heat and immediately begin to slowly pour the syrup mixture into the gelatin on low speed. Add the vanilla. Increase the mixer speed to high and mix for 3 to 4 minutes, or until the mixture is glossy and thick.

Spread the mixture in the prepared dish. Use damp hands or a spatula coated with coconut oil to easily spread the mixture. Let set for at least 4 hours. Cut into squares and store in an airtight container on the counter for 1 to 2 days, or freeze for up to 2 months.

Hormone-Balancing Chocolate Truffles

Chocolate is an important part of meal prep—shocking yet true! This batched chocolate dessert is delicious for everyone but especially helpful for menstruating folks to have on hand at the beginning of their cycle when the body craves the nutrients found in chocolate, such as magnesium. These pack an extra benefit with some maca powder, a powerful adaptogen that has been shown to support the endocrine system and healthy hormone production. When your menstrual phase comes around and you're craving a sweet, chocolaty treat, have these satisfying hormone-healthy truffles ready to grab in the fridge rather than leaning on ultraprocessed foods that could amplify your PMS symptoms. Meal prepping around your cycle is so important, especially since caloric needs go up during the luteal and menstrual phase, which coincidentally is the part of the phase when most people aren't feeling up to hours in the kitchen.

Yield: 8 truffles

2.5 oz (70 g) cacao butter

3 tbsp (18 g) unsweetened raw cacao powder

3 tbsp (45 g) maca powder

1½ tsp (4 g) ground cinnamon

3 tbsp (43 g) salted butter, at room temperature

2 tbsp (30 ml) pure maple syrup

In a double boiler, melt the cacao butter, 5 to 6 minutes, then set aside to cool slightly. If you don't have a double boiler, place a heatproof bowl atop a small pot partially filled with water, ensuring that the water does not touch the bottom of the bowl. Bring the water to a simmer over medium-low heat—the steam will melt the contents of the bowl without burning it.

Stir the cacao powder, maca powder and cinnamon into the melted cacao butter until fully combined. Stir in the butter until combined. Stir in the maple syrup. Pour into small molds and let set in the fridge until solid.

Store the truffles in the fridge in an airtight container for 1 to 2 weeks. To freeze, store in an airtight container for up to 3 months. Let them thaw for 20 minutes before serving.

Freezer-Friendly Mint Truffles

Have the nostalgic flavor of a peppermint patty in your freezer at all times with this homemade, naturally sweetened and whole food version. They are incredibly easy to put together and require only five ingredients. The coconut oil and cacao butter provide healthy fat that will help you feel satiated after eating this dessert.

Yield: 10 truffles

⅓ cup (73 g) coconut oil, at room temperature

1 tbsp (15 ml) raw honey, divided

15 to 20 drops peppermint extract

⅓ cup (53 g) cacao butter, melted

2½ tbsp (15 g) unsweetened raw cacao powder

In a bowl, combine the coconut oil, 1½ teaspoons (8 ml) of the honey and the peppermint extract, and stir to combine. Taste and add more peppermint or honey to reach your desired flavor. Divide into ten servings in a freezer mold and set in the freezer until solid, at least 30 minutes.

Once the peppermint mixture is set, make the chocolate coating: In a double boiler, melt the cacao butter. Remove from the heat and let it sit on the counter for 5 minutes to cool. Stir in the remaining 1½ teaspoons (8 ml) of honey and the cacao powder until incorporated. Let cool for 5 minutes.

One by one, dip each frozen mint patty into the bowl of chocolate and flip to coat. Set on a plate lined with parchment paper and return the patties to the freezer to set. Repeat one or two more times to completely coat the patties.

Let set in the freezer for a couple of minutes before enjoying. Store in an airtight container in the freezer for up to 3 months.

Grain-Free Frosted Pumpkin Bread

Not only is this pumpkin bread incredibly moist, flavorful and decadent, but it's grain-free, naturally sweetened and packed with healthy fat and some added protein! It's made with real, whole food ingredients so you can enjoy a delicious treat and feel great, too. During pumpkin season, make a few batches, slice them up and store in the freezer. You can toast a slice right from the freezer and top with the creamy frosting when you're ready to enjoy it.

Yield: 10 servings

Bread
½ cup (114 g/1 stick) unsalted butter

1 cup (245 g) pure pumpkin puree

1 tbsp (10 g) pumpkin pie spice

2 large eggs

1 tsp vanilla extract

1 tsp fresh lemon juice

1 large carrot, grated

⅓ cup (80 ml) pure maple syrup

½ cup (60 g) cassava flour

1 cup (85 g) unsweetened shredded coconut, blended into a fine flour

½ tsp baking soda

¼ tsp baking powder

¼ tsp sea salt

Frosting
½ cup (115 g) cottage cheese

½ cup (75 g) soft goat cheese

1 tbsp (15 ml) pure maple syrup

Preheat the oven to 350°F (180°C) and line an 8 x 4–inch (20 x 10–cm) loaf pan with parchment paper.

Start by browning the butter: In a small stainless-steel saucepan or skillet, cook the butter over medium heat, stirring continuously to prevent burning. After 6 to 7 minutes, or when the butter turns golden brown and smells nutty, remove from the heat and immediately transfer it to a heat-proof bowl (make sure to scrape all the flavorful brown bits out of the pan!).

In the same pan, combine the pumpkin puree and pumpkin pie spice and cook over medium heat, stirring frequently, until slightly thickened, about 4 minutes.

To the bowl of butter, add the eggs and vanilla, and stir to combine. Stir in the cooked-down pumpkin puree, lemon juice, grated carrot and maple syrup. Add the cassava flour, coconut flour, baking soda, baking powder and sea salt, and stir to combine.

Transfer the batter to the prepared loaf pan and bake for about 1 hour. It is ready when a knife inserted into the center comes out clean. Remove from the oven, remove the loaf from the pan and let it cool. If you are going to freeze the bread, do not frost the bread. If you are going to refrigerate the bread, once the bread is cool, make the frosting: In a blender, blend together the cottage cheese, goat cheese and maple syrup until smooth. Smooth the frosting over the loaf.

Store the bread in an airtight container in the fridge for 5 to 6 days. To freeze, line a baking sheet with parchment paper. Slice the unfrosted loaf and place the slices in a single layer on the lined baking sheet. Freeze until solid, then transfer to an airtight freezer-friendly container and freeze for up to 4 months.

Gluten-Free Fermented Banana Bread

Here is a delicious, moist banana bread without added sugar or unhealthy vegetable oils. This gluten-free banana bread starts with fermenting buckwheat overnight to improve digestibility. It's minimally sweetened with the ripe bananas and maple syrup. The secret weapon that keeps this loaf extra moist is the Greek yogurt, which also adds some extra nutrients and quality protein.

Yield: 10 servings

1 cup (170 g) raw buckwheat groats

1 cup (240 ml) warm water

3 large eggs, whisked

½ cup (115 g) plain Greek yogurt

1 tsp vanilla extract

⅓ cup (80 ml) pure maple syrup

3 very ripe bananas

1 cup (85 g) unsweetened shredded coconut, blended into a fine flour

1 tsp baking soda

½ tsp baking powder

¼ tsp sea salt

1 tsp ground cinnamon

¾ cup (126 g) chocolate chips, divided

In a blender, blend the buckwheat groats into a fine flour. In a medium-sized bowl, combine the buckwheat flour with the warm water. Cover with a clean dish towel and let sit in a warm place for 24 hours (I like to put mine in the warm laundry room to support fermentation).

After 24 hours of fermentation, preheat the oven to 350°F (180°C) and line a 9 x 5–inch (23 x 13–cm) loaf pan with parchment paper.

Whisk the eggs directly into the bowl of fermented buckwheat flour. Stir in the yogurt, vanilla and maple syrup. Mash in the bananas, leaving some larger chunks.

In a small bowl, combine the coconut flour, baking soda, baking powder, sea salt and cinnamon. Once thoroughly combined, add this mixture to the fermented buckwheat mixture and stir just enough to combine. Stir in ½ cup (84 g) of the chocolate chips. Transfer the mixture to the prepared pan and top with the remaining chocolate chips. Bake for 60 minutes, or until a knife inserted into the center comes out clean. Remove the bread from the oven and let it cool.

Store the bread in an airtight container in the fridge for 5 to 6 days. To freeze, line a baking sheet with parchment paper. Slice the loaf and place the slices in a single layer on the lined baking sheet. Freeze until solid, then transfer to an airtight freezer-friendly container and freeze for up to 4 months.

Grain-Free Chocolate Chip Cookies

A good grain-free cookie that isn't too dense or chalky is hard to come by. The secret to making grain-free cookies that you actually enjoy is the browned butter and tahini that give these cookies a complex nutty and sweet flavor. Whip up a batch, bake a few and store the rest in the freezer to have an easy, nutrient-dense cookie on hand.

Yield: 12 cookies

½ cup (114 g/1 stick) unsalted butter

¼ cup (60 ml) tahini

3 tbsp (45 ml) pure maple syrup

1 tsp vanilla extract

1 large egg

1 large egg yolk

½ cup (60 g) cassava flour

3 tbsp (24 g) tapioca flour

½ tsp baking soda

½ tsp sea salt

¾ cup (126 g) chocolate chips

Preheat the oven to 350°F (180°C).

Start by browning the butter: In a small stainless-steel saucepan or skillet, cook the butter over medium heat, stirring continuously to prevent burning. After 6 to 7 minutes, or when the butter turns golden brown and smells nutty, remove it from the heat and transfer immediately to a heat-proof bowl (make sure to scrape all the flavorful brown bits out of the pan).

Let the butter cool for 1 to 2 minutes, then add the tahini, maple syrup and vanilla, and stir until combined. Add the egg and egg yolk to the bowl and whisk for 1 to 2 minutes, or until the mixture is lighter in color and fluffy.

In another bowl, combine the cassava flour, tapioca flour, baking soda and sea salt and mix well. Add half of the flour mixture to the butter mixture and stir until combined. Add the remaining flour mixture and gently stir just until completely incorporated. Stir in the chocolate chips.

Divide the dough into balls slightly larger than the size of golf balls. Place them 2 inches (5 cm) apart on a parchment-lined baking sheet and lightly press down each dough ball to 1 inch (2.5-cm) thickness. Bake for 7 minutes, or until golden brown. Remove from the oven and let cool before enjoying.

To freeze, place the raw dough balls on a baking sheet lined with parchment paper and freeze until solid. Then, transfer the dough balls to an airtight container and freeze for 2 to 3 months. When you are ready to bake, thaw the dough in the fridge overnight, then let the dough sit out of the fridge for 30 minutes before following the above baking instructions.

Make-Ahead Hot Chocolate Bombs

When your sweet tooth hits, you can have a decadent, creamy hot chocolate in 60 seconds. These are naturally sweetened and packed with healthy fats to mitigate a blood sugar spike that can leave you feeling drained and craving more sugar. This is a hot chocolate that will actually fill you up and leave you satisfied! For a hot day, whip one up and pour it over ice for a creamy chocolate milk.

Yield: 12 chocolate bombs

6 Medjool dates, pitted

⅓ cup (80 g) coconut butter

2 tbsp (30 g) tahini

¼ tsp sea salt

1 tbsp (7 g) ground cinnamon

1 tsp vanilla extract

¾ cup (72 g) unsweetened raw cacao powder, plus more for coating

Soak the dates in hot water for 10 to 15 minutes until soft. Drain the water.

In a blender or food processor, combine the soaked dates, coconut butter, tahini, sea salt, cinnamon and vanilla, and blend until mostly mixed. Add the cacao powder and blend until smooth.

Use your hands to roll the mixture into small truffles. Roll each ball in cacao powder to coat and place on a baking sheet lined with parchment paper. Freeze until solid and then transfer to an airtight container. Store in the freezer for up to 3 months.

To make hot chocolate, heat ¾ cup (175 ml) of your milk of choice. Drop in one or two frozen bombs, depending on how rich you like your hot chocolate, and stir until melted. You can also blend the bombs into the warm milk for an extra-frothy hot cocoa.

Single-Serving Key Lime Pie

This dessert is like a flavor bomb in your mouth—sweet, nutty crust, topped with a creamy tart filling and fresh whipped cream. It's everything we love about Key lime pie, but with much less sugar, naturally gluten-free, and can be made dairy-free if needed. This recipe makes five single servings that can be eaten right away, or store them in the freezer and thaw when you want a taste of summer on a Florida beach! For easy storage, assemble these directly in a small Mason jar that you can add a lid to.

Yield: 5 servings

½ cup (67 g) raw macadamia nuts

½ cup (50 g) raw pecans

1 date, pitted

Pinch of sea salt

½ cup (120 m) fresh lime juice (Key lime or regular lime works.)

1 medium-sized avocado, peeled, pitted and cubed

1 tbsp (15 ml) raw honey or pure maple syrup

2 tbsp (30 ml) coconut cream

¼ tsp vanilla extract

2 tbsp (30 g) coconut butter

¼ tsp spirulina powder (optional)

½ cup (120 ml) cold heavy cream or coconut cream

½ tsp vanilla extract

In a food processor or blender, combine the macadamia nuts, pecans, date and sea salt, and blend until the nuts are finely chopped and have combined with the date. The mixture should be crumbly but stick together when you press it together in your hand. Divide the mixture equally among five 4-ounce (120-ml) Mason jars, using clean hands or the back of a spoon to push it down into a solid crust.

In a clean blender or food processor, combine the lime juice, avocado, honey, coconut cream and vanilla, and blend for 20 to 30 seconds, or until just mixed. Add the coconut butter and spirulina powder (if using), then blend until smooth and fully combined. Divide the mixture equally among the jars.

Make the homemade whipped cream topping: In a large bowl or the bowl of a stand mixer, combine the heavy cream and vanilla, then use an electric hand mixer or the stand mixer fitted with the whisk attachment to whisk on high speed, about 1 minute, until medium-stiff peaks form. Divide the mixture equally among the jars.

Seal each jar with a lid and store in the fridge for 3 to 4 days. To freeze, store in the freezer for up to 3 months. When ready to serve, thaw in the fridge until soft.

Sauces and Condiments

The first thing that I tell people who are trying to incorporate a more nutrient-dense way of eating is to audit their condiments. Sauces, dressings and condiments are commonly sources of added sugars, unhealthy fats and other unhealthy additives, such as chemical preservatives. In this chapter, you will find a variety of flavorful sauces and condiments that use healthy fats, including extra virgin olive oil and quality dairy; contain nutrient-rich herbs and spices and are very minimally and naturally sweetened, so your condiments aren't sneaking hidden sugars into your diet. My 5-Ingredient Mayonnaise (page 143) is such an important swap in so many homes—it takes 60 seconds to whip up a healthy mayo that tastes better than store-bought mayo full of inflammatory oils. The Bone Marrow Butter (page 157) is a decadent treat to make and a great way to incorporate nutrient-rich bone marrow into your diet.

5-Ingredient Mayonnaise

I used to despise mayonnaise, but then I made fresh mayo at home and my life changed. The problem with most store-bought mayonnaises is that they are made with poor-quality, inflammatory seed oils. Having a batch of quality mayo in your fridge means you can leave the poor-quality mayo in the past. Use this to keep a sandwich moist, make a quality chicken or egg salad, thicken up a salad dressing and so much more! Avocado oil is a neutral oil that will give you the traditional mayo flavor. If you like the taste of olive oil, you can use a mild olive oil, although some people think it can be bitter. Or use a combo of avocado and olive oil!

Yield: 2 cups (450 g)

---

1 large egg

1 tsp Dijon mustard

1 tsp apple cider vinegar

¼ tsp sea salt

1 cup (240 ml) avocado oil or mild extra virgin olive oil

A few hours before making the mayonnaise, pull your ingredients out of the fridge to let them come to room temperature. If you forget to do this, put the egg in a bowl of warm water for a few minutes before making the mayonnaise.

Crack the egg into a wide-mouth 8-ounce (240-ml) Mason jar or similarly shaped container, being careful to not break the yolk. Add the mustard, apple cider vinegar and sea salt. Do not mix or stir. Pour the oil into the jar.

Slowly lower an immersion blender into the jar until it reaches the bottom of the jar. Blend on low speed until the mixture has turned mostly white—this should take about 10 seconds. Then, slowly raise the blender, still running it, without removing it from the mixture. Once you reach the top of the mixture, slowly move the blender back to the bottom. Repeat this up-and-down motion a few times until the mayonnaise thickens.

Cover with a tight lid. The mayonnaise can be stored in the fridge for 10 to 14 days.

Probiotic-Rich Salsa

Salsa is a great way to add vibrant veggies and flavor to any meal. This salsa is lacto-fermented, meaning you're also getting gut-healthy probiotic bacteria into your diet. Fermentation is a great way to extend the shelf life of food—make a huge batch in the summer, when tomatoes are plentiful, and preserve the fresh flavors of summer in your fridge through winter! Add it to rice bowls with the Gut-Friendly Herb Rice (page 74), use it on tacos using the Family-Size Pork Carnitas (page 55) or serve it as a snack for a boost of gut-health support!

Yield: 12 servings

1 lb (455 g) Roma tomatoes, diced

1 jalapeño pepper, diced (remove the seeds for reduced spice)

1 bell pepper, seeded and diced

1 red onion, diced

5 cloves garlic, peeled and minced

½ cup (8 g) fresh cilantro, chopped

Juice of 2 limes

1 tbsp (18 g) sea salt

In a large bowl, combine the tomatoes, peppers, red onion, garlic, cilantro, lime juice and sea salt, and stir well to distribute them evenly.

Divide equally between two 24-ounce (710-ml) Mason jars and add a nonmetal fermentation weight to each to keep the ingredients submerged in juices. Top with a fermentation lid or a loose lid, and let sit on the counter for 2 to 3 days. If your house is especially warm, it may be ready closer to 1 to 2 days.

While the salsa ferments, check each day to ensure the veggies stay below the liquid.

Taste the salsa each day. Once you have achieved your desired flavor, remove the fermentation weights, secure each lid tightly and transfer the jars to the fridge. Store in the fridge for 3 to 4 months.

Spicy Cilantro Sauce

Creamy, spicy sauce with quality protein and some science-backed health benefits? Yes, please! The base of this sauce is cottage cheese, which makes it creamy and smooth but also provides some quality protein. Cilantro is known to bind to heavy metals in the body and support detoxification, and it may even support heart health. The jalapeño and lime bring some kick and brightness to the sauce. This is the perfect pair for my Make-and-Freeze Kebabs (page 52), any other meat dish, or even as a dipping sauce for veggies or the base of a salad dressing. This is the perfect sauce to prep for a week so that you can spice up any leftover dish with a drizzle!

Yield: 12 servings

1 bunch cilantro

Juice of 1 lime

1 jalapeño pepper (remove the seeds for reduced spice)

¾ cup (169 g) cottage cheese

4 cloves garlic, peeled

½ avocado, peeled and pitted

1 tsp sea salt

In a blender or food processor, combine the cilantro, lime juice, jalapeño, cottage cheese, garlic, avocado and sea salt, and blend until smooth. Add water if you want to thin the sauce.

Store in an airtight container in the fridge for up to 7 days.

Everyday Vinaigrette Dressing

Stock your fridge each week with fresh dressing and never buy store-bought dressing again! Salad dressing can seem like an innocuous option on the grocery shelves, but most are made with refined, inflammatory seed oils, unnecessary added sugar and chemical preservatives. You can have a much more delicious and fresh option at home that is made with quality fats and real food ingredients with some simple pantry and fridge staples. You can use this simple recipe as is or use it as a base to experiment with extra spices, different acids and even seasonal fruit additions!

Yield: 1 cup (240ml)

¾ cup (175 ml) extra virgin olive oil

¼ cup (60 ml) acid of choice (fresh lemon juice, apple cider vinegar, red wine vinegar, etc.)

1 clove garlic, minced

1 tsp Dijon mustard or mayonnaise

1 tsp raw honey (optional)

½ tsp sea salt

In a small bowl, combine the olive oil, your acid of choice, garlic, mustard, honey (if using) and sea salt, and whisk together. Alternatively, combine them in a jar, seal with a lid and shake vigorously.

Serve immediately or save in the fridge for up to 2 weeks.

* The Everyday Vinaigrette Dressing is shown in the back left jar in the photo.

Probiotic-Rich Salad Dressing

This is one of my favorite dressing recipes because it's great for the gut and a great way to avoid food waste. A fermentation brine is the liquid used to ferment—it is tangy and full of the gut-healthy bacteria that we love in ferments. Most people enjoy their sauerkraut or kimchi and toss the liquid that remains at the bottom of the jar. Instead, this is the perfect ingredient to use as the acid in your dressing. Bonus: If you have an empty ferment jar with some remaining brine at the bottom, you can make the dressing right in that jar for a no-mess recipe.

Yield: 1 cup (240ml)

¾ cup (175 ml) extra virgin olive oil

¼ cup (60 ml) sauerkraut or kimchi brine

1 tsp Dijon mustard

2 cloves garlic, minced

½ tsp sea salt

In a bowl, combine the olive oil, brine, mustard, garlic and sea salt, and whisk together. Alternatively, combine them in a jar, seal with a lid and shake vigorously.

Serve immediately or save in the fridge for up to 2 weeks.

* The Probiotic-Rich Salad Dressing is shown in the front jar in the image on page 149.

Creamy Caesar Dip

I have never eaten salad so quickly and with such few complaints. Caesar dressing gets a bad rap because of the poor ingredients and additives in your typical store-bought version. This homemade dressing is packed with flavor without the harmful vegetable oils or additives. Don't limit this to your salads, though—prep a big batch to keep in your fridge, and use this as a dip for my Perfect Roasted Veggies (page 83)—you'll be shocked how quickly the veggies go. P.S. Don't be afraid of anchovies! They are a key part of this dressing. They don't impart a fishy flavor; they're just a great way to add salt to a sauce or dish. They are also a nutrient-dense food, rich in omega-3 fatty acids, vitamins B_3 and B_{12}, selenium, iron and calcium.

Yield: 1 cup (240 ml)

2 small cloves garlic, grated

3 to 4 anchovies, minced finely

2 tbsp (30 ml) fresh lemon juice

1 tsp Dijon mustard

½ cup (115 g) 5-Ingredient Mayonnaise (page 143)

½ cup (50 g) freshly grated Parmigiano-Reggiano cheese

Freshly ground black pepper

In a large bowl, whisk together the garlic, anchovies, lemon juice and mustard. Add the mayonnaise and Parmigiano-Reggiano, and whisk to combine. Season with pepper to taste.

Store the dressing in an airtight container in the fridge for 7 to 10 days.

* The Creamy Caesar Dip is shown in the back right jar in the image on page 149.

Budget-Friendly Pesto

I love pesto. I don't think there are many sauces that are better. The only problem is that it can be really pricey. A ton of fresh basil and pine nuts are some of the more expensive ingredients in the grocery store. This pesto has the same amazing flavor but cuts down on the cost by swapping out half of the basil for another leafy green while keeping it simple and nut-free. This pesto goes great with the Nutrient-Rich Liver Meatballs (page 38).

Yield: 1½ cups (355 ml)

2 cups (90 g) tightly packed basil leaves

1 cup (20 g) carrot tops or arugula

2 cloves garlic, peeled

½ tsp sea salt, plus more to taste

1 tbsp (15 ml) fresh lemon juice

½ cup (120 ml) extra virgin olive oil, plus more to top

½ cup (50 g) freshly grated Parmesan cheese

In a food processor or blender, combine the basil, carrot tops, garlic, sea salt and lemon juice and blend until roughly mixed. While the food processor or blender is running, slowly pour in the extra virgin olive oil through the center chute.

Add the Parmesan and blend until just incorporated. Taste the pesto and add more sea salt if needed.

Store in an airtight container in the fridge up to 5 days. To keep the pesto fresh longer, cover with a layer of olive oil. To freeze, divide into desired portion sizes and store in an airtight container for up to 6 months. When you're ready to use the pesto, just thaw in the fridge for 3 to 4 hours or until soft enough to use.

Simple Fruit Jam

This simple fruit spread is a great way to enjoy the sweet bursts of flavor of jam without tons of added sugar or preservatives typically found in store-bought versions. Choose your berry of choice or do a mixture of berries and customize the sweetness by adding sweetener to taste! This is also a great way to preserve fruits at their peak to enjoy later in the year when fresh berries are not in season.

Yield: 1½ cups (320 g)

---

20 oz (567 g/about 3 cups) frozen berries of choice

1 tbsp (15 ml) fresh lime juice

½ tsp grass-fed beef gelatin powder

1 to 2 tbsp (15 to 30 ml) pure maple syrup or raw honey (optional)

Place the fruit in a medium-sized saucepan. Add in the fresh lime juice. Cover and cook over medium-low heat, stirring occasionally and use a wooden spoon to smash the fruit. Cook for 20 to 25 minutes, or until the fruit is cooked down. Sprinkle in the gelatin powder and cook for another 3 minutes. Taste and add maple syurp or raw honey if you prefer a sweeter jam.

Remove from the heat and transfer to a glass jar with a lid. Let cool, then place in the fridge until set, 2 to 3 hours. Store in an airtight container in the fridge for 7 to 10 days. To freeze, divide into desired portion sizes and store in an airtight container for up to 6 months. When ready to use, simply thaw in the fridge overnight.

Bone Marrow Butter

This spread feels decadent and indulgent, but it's also packed with valuable nutrients. Bone marrow has been consumed in many cuisines for thousands of years. It is rich in collagen—the most abundant protein in your body—which promotes skin and joint health. Combined with softened butter, this is a delicious way to incorporate nutrients that a typical diet might be missing and a good dose of healthy fats. It is very rich, so a little bit goes a long way, making this spread a great fridge staple. Add a pat to meat dishes, spread it on toast or use it to cook your eggs—the options are endless!

Yield: 16 servings

---

4 marrow bones, cut lengthwise

Sea salt

1 head garlic, cut in half

½ cup (114 g/1 stick) salted butter, at room temperature

Soak the bones 12 to 24 hours before roasting: Fill a large bowl halfway with ice water plus 1 tablespoon (18 g) of sea salt. Add the marrow bones and refrigerate for 12 to 24 hours. This is not necessary, but will remove any impurities from the bone marrow.

When you are ready to roast the bones, preheat the oven to 450°F (230°C). Remove the butter from the fridge to let it soften.

Drain and rinse the bones, then dry them thoroughly. Season the marrow bones with a sprinkle of sea salt. Place the marrow bones, cut side up, in a roasting pan. Place the garlic, cut side down, in the pan. Roast for 15 to 25 minutes. The marrow should easily come away from the bones when it is done.

Scrape the marrow from the bones and set aside in a bowl to cool for 10 minutes.

To the bowl of bone marrow, add the softened butter and squeeze the roasted garlic cloves from the head of garlic. Use a fork or whisk to mix it all together until the bone marrow and garlic cloves are broken down and everything is well combined. Taste and add sea salt to your preference.

Store in an airtight container in the fridge for up to 7 days, or freeze for up to 6 months. The butter will firm up in the fridge, so when you're ready to serve, let it come to room temperature and whisk the butter for a creamy texture.

Chimichurri

Chimichurri is an herb sauce originally from Argentina and Uruguay. It's a common topping for meat dishes, but it's deliciously versatile and a great way to add fresh herbs to other meals. It requires zero cooking, just a bit of chopping and time for the herbs to marinate in the oil and vinegar to develop their flavors. That's the best part—it gets better with time as it sits in the fridge for the week, or you can freeze it in small portions so that you always have some fresh, herby flavor on hand. Plus, it's a great way to use those wilting herbs that you forgot were sitting in the back of your fridge.

Yield: 8 servings

1 bunch parsley, chopped finely

4 cloves garlic, chopped finely

1 to 2 Fresno chiles, chopped finely

1 tsp dried oregano

1 cup (240 ml) extra virgin olive oil

¼ cup (60 ml) red wine vinegar

½ tsp sea salt

Freshly ground black pepper

In a bowl, combine the parsley, garlic, chiles and oregano. Pour the olive oil and vinegar over all the ingredients and mix well. Add more olive oil as needed. The parsley should be well coated.

Let the mixture sit for 1 to 2 hours to let the flavors develop. Taste and season with salt and black pepper to your liking.

Store in an airtight container in the fridge for 2 to 3 weeks. To freeze, divide into desired portions and freeze in an airtight container for 3 to 4 months. When you're ready to use, let it thaw in the fridge overnight. Refresh it with a dash of olive oil and vinegar to thin out the sauce, if needed.

Fermented Hot Sauce

This homemade hot sauce is the perfect balance of spicy and sweet, thanks to the juicy peaches. Fermentation brings the hot sauce to a whole new level of intricate flavors. You can also use this formula to play around with different fruit and pepper combinations. With this recipe, you will make the most delicious and healthiest hot sauce to level up any dish!

Yield: 5 cups (1.2 L)

3 peaches (470 g), chopped roughly

¾ lb (300 g) Fresno peppers, roughly chopped

4 cloves garlic (30 g), peeled and roughly chopped

2 tbsp (9 g) fresh ginger, roughly chopped

½ red onion (140 g), roughly chopped

3 cups (720 ml) filtered water

3 tbsp + ½ tsp (58 g) sea salt

⅓ cup (80 ml) apple cider vinegar

In a 64-ounce (1.9-L) Mason jar, combine the peaches, Fresno peppers, garlic, ginger and red onion.

Measure out the filtered water in a large bowl and mix in the sea salt. Stir until completely dissolved.

Add the salt water brine to the jar. Add a nonmetal fermentation weight to ensure all the ingredients stay below the water. Add an airlock lid or a Mason jar lid, and set in a place away from direct sunlight to ferment. Let sit for 2 to 3 weeks. If you're using a Mason jar lid, open the jar daily to burp the jar.

After 2 weeks of fermentation, you can start to taste the hot sauce to see if it has reached your desired flavor. After 2 to 3 weeks, once you have reached a flavor you like, drain the hot sauce, reserving the brine. Add the fermented mixture to a blender with ½ cup (120 ml) of the brine and ⅓ cup (80 ml) of apple cider vinegar, and blend until smooth. Taste and add more brine for a spicier sauce, or vinegar for a tangier flavor. Transfer to an airtight container and store in the fridge for up to 6 months.

Acknowledgments

A big thank-you to farmers and ranchers, who work tirelessly to provide us with nutritious food and healthy soil that we all rely on every day.

Thanks to my mentor, Diana Rodgers, for being a wealth of knowledge in nutrient-density and real food nutrition.

I would like to express my gratitude to Page Street Publishing; my editor, Franny Donington; and my photographer, Anne Watson, for bringing this project to life.

And finally, thanks to my partner, Sam, for being the perfect taste tester—critical but supportive.

About the Author

Olivia is a nutritional therapy practitioner (NTP) specializing in gut and hormone health. She helps women reclaim their health and vitality through delicious, nourishing food.

After healing her own chronic digestive issues and severe hormone imbalance through a nutrient-dense diet and lifestyle, she turned to educating others on the power they have in their kitchen. Through simple recipes and meal prep ideas, she makes cooking nutritious meals fun and accessible. She delivers online learning materials, meal prep support and new recipes every week to her online community.

Index

A

A2 dairy, 11

B

Balanced Smoothie
Formula, 103
Banana Bread, Gluten-Free
Fermented, 133
Batched Shepherd's Pie, 56
beef
Batched Shepherd's Pie,
56
Beef Tongue Birria,
49–51
Comforting Short Rib
Ragu, 46–48
Make-and-Freeze
Kebabs, 52
Mini Meat Muffins, 100
My Hearty Organ Meat
Chili, 41
Nutrient-Rich Liver
Meatballs, 38
Simplified Bone Broth, 30
Thai Larb Lettuce Cups,
42
Beef Heart Jerky,
Nourishing, 45
Beef Tongue Birria, 49–51
Beet Salad, Heart-Healthy,
92
bell peppers
Mini Meat Muffins, 100
Probiotic-Rich Salsa, 144

Birria, Beef Tongue, 49–51
Bone Broth, Simplified, 30
Bone Broth Braised Greens,
88
Bone Broth Breakfast Soup,
5-Minute, 104
Bone Marrow Butter, 157
Bread, Gluten-Free
Fermented Banana, 133
Bread, Gluten-Free
Sourdough Sandwich, 65
Bread, Grain-Free Frosted
Pumpkin, 130
Breakfast Fried Rice, 111
Breakfast Parfait, Cottage
Cheese, 112
breakfasts, 97–117
Balanced Smoothie
Formula, 103
Breakfast Fried Rice, 111
Clean-the-Fridge Omelet,
116
Cottage Cheese
Breakfast Parfait, 112
5-Minute Bone Broth
Breakfast Soup, 104
High-Protein Pancakes,
115
Make-Ahead Protein
Oatmeal, 108
Mini Meat Muffins, 100
Savory Masa Bowl, 107
Single-Serving Frittata,
99
Budget-Friendly Pesto, 153
Butter, Bone Marrow, 157

C

Caesar Dip, Creamy, 151
carbohydrates, 63–79
Cheesy Scalloped
Potatoes, 66
Creamy Squash Soup, 78
Fresh Corn Tortillas, 77
Gluten-Free Sourdough
Sandwich Bread, 65
Gut-Friendly Herb Rice,
74
Middle Eastern Lentil
Salad, 70
Prebiotic Potato Salad,
69
Winter Squash Mash, 73
Carnitas, Family-Size Pork,
55
carrots
Batched Shepherd's Pie,
56
Comforting Short Rib
Ragu, 46–48
Perfect Roasted Veggies,
83
Simple Dill Carrot Salad,
95
Thai Larb Lettuce Cups,
42
cauliflower
Cheesy Scalloped
Potatoes, 66
Perfect Roasted Veggies,
83

celery
   Batched Shepherd's Pie,
   56
   Comforting Short Rib
   Ragu, 46–48
cheese. See also cottage
   cheese
   Batched Shepherd's Pie,
   56
   Cheesy Scalloped
   Potatoes, 66
   Clean-the-Fridge Omelet,
   116
   Make-and-Freeze
   Kebabs, 52
   Middle Eastern Lentil
   Salad, 70
   Mini Meat Muffins, 100
Cheesy Scalloped Potatoes,
66
chicken
   Easy Roasted Chicken, 34
   15-Minute Chicken Liver
   Mousse, 29
   Nutrient-Rich Liver
   Meatballs, 38
   Simple Curry Chicken
   Salad, 37
   Simplified Bone Broth, 30
Chicken Liver Mousse,
   15-Minute, 29
Chicken Salad, Simple
   Curry, 37
Chili, My Hearty Organ
   Meat, 41
Chimichurri, 157
Chocolate Bombs, Make-
   Ahead Hot, 137
Chocolate Chip Cookies,
   Grain-Free, 134

Chocolate Truffles,
   Hormone-Balancing, 126
Cilantro Sauce, Spicy, 147
Clean-the-Fridge Omelet,
   116
Comforting Short Rib Ragu,
   46–48
community supported
   agriculture (CSA), 12
Cookies, Grain-Free
   Chocolate Chip, 134
Corn Tortillas, Fresh, 77
cottage cheese
   Balanced Smoothie
   Formula, 103
   Cottage Cheese
   Breakfast Parfait, 112
   High-Protein Pancakes,
   115
   High-Protein Pot de
   Crème, 121
   Single-Serving Frittata,
   99
   Spicy Cilantro Sauce, 147
Cottage Cheese Breakfast
   Parfait, 112
Creamy Caesar Dip, 151
Creamy Nutrient-Dense Ice
   Cream, 122
Creamy Squash Soup, 78
Curry, Seafood Red, 59
Curry Chicken Salad,
   Simple, 37

D

dairy, sourcing, 11
desserts, 119–39
   Creamy Nutrient-Dense
   Ice Cream, 122

Freezer-Friendly Mint
   Truffles, 129
Gluten-Free Fermented
   Banana Bread, 133
Grain-Free Chocolate
   Chip Cookies, 134
Grain-Free Frosted
   Pumpkin Bread, 130
Gut-Healing Maple
   Marshmallows, 125
High-Protein Pot de
   Crème, 121
Hormone-Balancing
   Chocolate Truffles, 126
Make-Ahead Hot
   Chocolate Bombs, 137
Single-Serving Key Lime
   Pie, 138
Dill Carrot Salad, Simple, 95

E

Easy 30-Minute Sauerkraut,
   84
Easy Roasted Chicken, 34
eggs
   Breakfast Fried Rice, 111
   Clean-the-Fridge Omelet,
   116
   5-Minute Bone Broth
   Breakfast Soup, 104
   Make-Ahead Protein
   Oatmeal, 108
   Single-Serving Frittata,
   99
   Turmeric Pickled Eggs,
   33
Everyday Vinaigrette
   Dressing, 148

F

Family-Size Pork Carnitas, 55

Fermented Banana Bread, Gluten-Free, 133

fermented dairy, 11

Fermented Hot Sauce, 161

15-Minute Chicken Liver Mousse, 29

5-Ingredient Mayonnaise, 143

5-Minute Bone Broth Breakfast Soup, 104

Freezer-Friendly Mint Truffles, 129

French Ratatouille, Rustic, 91

Fresh Corn Tortillas, 77

Fried Rice, Breakfast, 111

Frittata, Single-Serving, 99

Fruit Jam, Simple, 154

G

Gluten-Free Fermented Banana Bread, 133

Gluten-Free Sourdough Sandwich Bread, 65

Grain-Free Chocolate Chip Cookies, 134

Grain-Free Frosted Pumpkin Bread, 130

Greens, Bone Broth Braised, 88

Gut-Friendly Herb Rice, 74

Gut-Healing Maple Marshmallows, 125

H

Heart-Healthy Beet Salad, 92

Herb Rice, Gut-Friendly, 74

High-Protein Pancakes, 115

High-Protein Pot de Crème, 121

Hormone-Balancing Chocolate Truffles, 126

Hot Chocolate Bombs, Make-Ahead, 137

Hot Sauce, Fermented, 161

I

Ice Cream, Creamy Nutrient-Dense, 122

ingredients, sourcing, 9–12

J

Jam, Simple Fruit, 154

Jerky, Nourishing Beef Heart, 45

K

Kebabs, Make-and-Freeze, 52

Key Lime Pie, Single-Serving, 138

L

Lacto-Fermented Veggies, 87

Larb Lettuce Cups, Thai, 42

Lentil Salad, Middle Eastern, 70

Lettuce Cups, Thai Larb, 42

Liver Meatballs, Nutrient-Rich, 38

local produce, 12

M

Make-Ahead Hot Chocolate Bombs, 137

Make-Ahead Protein Oatmeal, 108

Make-and-Freeze Kebabs, 52

Maple Marshmallows, Gut-Healing, 125

Maple Salmon Bites, 60

Marshmallows, Gut-Healing Maple, 125

Masa Bowl, Savory, 107

Mayonnaise, 5-Ingredient, 143

meal plans, 15–25

meal prep guide, 13

meat, sourcing, 10–11. See also proteins

Meat Muffins, Mini, 100

Middle Eastern Lentil Salad, 70

Mini Meat Muffins, 100

Mint Truffles, Freezer-Friendly, 129

Muffins, Mini Meat, 100

mushrooms

Mini Meat Muffins, 100

Thai Larb Lettuce Cups, 42

My Hearty Organ Meat Chili, 41

N

Nourishing Beef Heart Jerky, 45

nutrient density, 9

Nutrient-Rich Liver Meatballs, 38

O

Oatmeal, Make-Ahead
Protein, 108
Organ Meat Chili, My
Hearty, 41

P

Pancakes, High-Protein, 115
Parfait, Cottage Cheese
Breakfast, 112
Perfect Roasted Veggies, 83
Pesto, Budget-Friendly, 153
Pickled Eggs, Turmeric, 33
pork
Family-Size Pork
Carnitas, 55
Nutrient-Rich Liver
Meatballs, 38
Thai Larb Lettuce Cups,
42
Pork Carnitas, Family-Size,
55
potatoes
Batched Shepherd's Pie,
56
Cheesy Scalloped
Potatoes, 66
Prebiotic Potato Salad,
69
Potato Salad, Prebiotic, 69
Pot de Crème, High-Protein,
121
Prebiotic Potato Salad, 69
Probiotic-Rich Salad
Dressing, 150
Probiotic-Rich Salsa, 144
produce, sourcing, 12
Protein Oatmeal, Make-
Ahead, 108

proteins, 27–61
Batched Shepherd's Pie,
56
Beef Tongue Birria,
49–51
Comforting Short Rib
Ragu, 46–48
Easy Roasted Chicken, 34
Family-Size Pork
Carnitas, 55
15-Minute Chicken Liver
Mousse, 29
Make-and-Freeze
Kebabs, 52
Maple Salmon Bites, 60
My Hearty Organ Meat
Chili, 41
Nourishing Beef Heart
Jerky, 45
Nutrient-Rich Liver
Meatballs, 38
Seafood Red Curry, 59
Simple Curry Chicken
Salad, 37
Simplified Bone Broth, 30
sourcing meat, 10–11
Thai Larb Lettuce Cups,
42
Turmeric Pickled Eggs,
33
Pumpkin Bread, Grain-Free
Frosted, 130

R

Ragu, Comforting Short Rib,
46–48
Ratatouille, Rustic French,
91
Red Curry, Seafood, 59

rice
Breakfast Fried Rice, 111
Gut-Friendly Herb Rice,
74
Roasted Chicken, Easy, 34
Roasted Veggies, Perfect,
83
Rustic French Ratatouille,
91

S

Salad Dressing, Probiotic-
Rich, 150
Salmon Bites, Maple, 60
Salsa, Probiotic-Rich, 144
Sandwich Bread, Gluten-
Free Sourdough, 65
sauces and condiments,
141–61
Bone Marrow Butter, 157
Budget-Friendly Pesto,
153
Chimichurri, 157
Creamy Caesar Dip, 151
Everyday Vinaigrette
Dressing, 148
Fermented Hot Sauce,
161
5-Ingredient Mayonnaise,
143
Probiotic-Rich Salad
Dressing, 150
Probiotic-Rich Salsa, 144
Simple Fruit Jam, 154
Spicy Cilantro Sauce, 147
Sauerkraut, Easy
30-Minute, 84
Savory Masa Bowl, 107
Seafood Red Curry, 59
seasonal produce, 12

Shepherd's Pie, Batched, 56
Short Rib Ragu, Comforting, 46–48
Simple Curry Chicken Salad, 37
Simple Dill Carrot Salad, 95
Simple Fruit Jam, 154
Simplified Bone Broth, 30
Single-Serving Frittata, 99
Single-Serving Key Lime Pie, 138
Smoothie Formula, Balanced, 103
sourcing ingredients, 9–12
Sourdough Sandwich Bread, Gluten-Free, 65
Spicy Cilantro Sauce, 147
squash
    Creamy Squash Soup, 78
    Rustic French Ratatouille, 91
    Winter Squash Mash, 73
sweet potato
    My Hearty Organ Meat Chili, 41
    Perfect Roasted Veggies, 83

T
Thai Larb Lettuce Cups, 42
tomatoes
    Beef Tongue Birria, 49–51
    Comforting Short Rib Ragu, 46–48
    Middle Eastern Lentil Salad, 70
    My Hearty Organ Meat Chili, 41
    Probiotic-Rich Salsa, 144
    Rustic French Ratatouille, 91
Tortillas, Fresh Corn, 77
Truffles, Freezer-Friendly Mint, 129
Truffles, Hormone-Balancing Chocolate, 126
Turmeric Pickled Eggs, 33

V
vegetables, 81–95
    Bone Broth Braised Greens, 88
    Easy 30-Minute
    Sauerkraut, 84
    Heart-Healthy Beet Salad, 92
    Lacto-Fermented Veggies, 87
    Perfect Roasted Veggies, 83
    Rustic French Ratatouille, 91
    Simple Dill Carrot Salad, 95
Vinaigrette Dressing, Everyday, 148

W
Winter Squash Mash, 73

Z
zucchini
    My Hearty Organ Meat Chili, 41
    Rustic French Ratatouille, 91